Getting
More Business

Getting
More Business

*Use proven marketing techniques
and get business coming to you*

SALLYANN SHERIDAN

How To Books

Published by How To Books Ltd,
3 Newtec Place, Magdalen Road,
Oxford OX4 1RE, United Kingdom.
Tel: 01865 793806. Fax: 01865 248780.
email: info@howtobooks.co.uk
http://www.howtobooks.co.uk

British Library Cataloguing in Publication Data.
A catalogue record for this book is available from
the British Library.

Cover design by Shireen Nathoo Design
Cover copy Sallyann Sheridan
Cover image PhotoDisc
Cartoons by Mike Flanagan

Produced for How To Books by Deer Park Productions
Typeset by PDQ Typesetting, Newcastle-under-Lyme, Staffs.
Printed and bound by Cromwell Press, Trowbridge, Wiltshire

NOTE: The material contained in this book is set out in good
faith for general guidance and no liability can be accepted
for loss or expense incurred as a result of relying in particular
circumstances on statements made in the book. Laws and
regulations are complex and liable to change, and readers should
check the current position with the relevant authorities before
making personal arrangements.

Contents

5

Preface

"Everything you do is marketing."

Marketing. The word may fill you with dread, but everything you do is marketing – from the way you answer the phone to the words you write in your adverts. If you're self-employed or run a small- to medium-sized business, I wrote this book for you. The proven techniques and examples used throughout can be interpreted in thousands of ways to suit your business.

Many of the techniques apply equally to large corporations, but you have two major advantages – you can make them truly personal, and start using them today. But this book doesn't just show you proven ways to get more business coming to you, it helps you decide if what you're offering is easily marketable – and what steps to take if not.

You know more about your business than anyone else, which makes you the best person to market it. But, as this book reveals, marketing isn't something you do when you have time, it's something you make time for if you want to be successful and profitable. Market passionately and remember, the greatest risk you can take is to do nothing.

I wish you every success.

Sallyann Sheridan

Stephen, ce livre est pour toi, avec beaucoup
d'amour et je te remercie mille fois.

1

Who Are Your Customers and What Do They Buy?

Whether you're already in business, just starting out, self-employed, in a partnership, or run or own a small- to medium-sized company, the *principles* of getting more business are the same. But before putting these proven techniques into practice it helps to take a look at exactly what it is you're selling and focus on who you're selling it to. Business is all about people. You buy from people, not suppliers, and sell to people, not businesses. The term *selling business to business* is rapidly leaving the marketer's vocabulary, because it's people you have to connect with successfully if you're going to make that sale.

> **Ask not what your customers can do for you,
> but what you can do for them.**

CHECKING YOUR PRODUCT OR SERVICE

Is your product or service easy to market?
Every product is marketable, but if you have one which is easily marketable it will make getting more business that much simpler. Does your product or service lend itself to a range of marketing techniques – direct mail, special offers, bonuses? Consultancies and service industries are examples of businesses that fit into this category, and include services such as training, garage repairs and information services.

> **One thing is for sure, when you have an excellent product
> or service, marketing is much easier.**

Is there really a gap in the market?

Perhaps you're going into business because you noticed a gap in the market – a niche that you could fill. But perhaps the gap was there for a good reason. Maybe others tried selling in this area without success. In other words, there may be a gap in the market because *there isn't a market in the gap.* Don't make assumptions – if others have tried the same business and not made it, talk to them and find out why. Offer them a fee for their time if necessary. They might highlight something which you have overlooked, or couldn't possibly have considered, and save you thousands of pounds into the bargain. Or maybe they didn't succeed because their product or service isn't as good as yours. Either way, you'll be far more informed.

Are you concentrating only on what you're good at?

Many people choose to go into business because they're good at something – computer training, plumbing or accountancy, for example. Perhaps you work in the building trade, an estate agents, clothes or DIY shop, and think you could run a similar business having learned the ins and outs of the trade. It isn't enough to be good at what you do, however, you've got to get to grips with marketing. And, in the early days of your business especially, you can expect to spend at least half your time and effort simply on getting business.

Do people want or need what you offer?

Do you have a product or service that people need, or one that people want? It's not enough for people to need what you offer, they have to want it.

> **All marketing has to be directed at what people want –
> not what they need.**

Are repeat sales possible?

Something else worth considering is whether you can offer repeat sales of your product or service. If you supply and fit double-glazed windows and doors which have a 25-year guarantee, for example, these are one-off sales, so it's unlikely you'll make repeat sales to the same customer. This means you have to constantly seek new customers. Consider the difference between this example and antique dealers, hairdressers or financial advisers – all these can sell to the same customer over and over again. If you are in the position of having a once-only-sale product or service, you could consider offering associated products as a way of doing repeat business.

What is unique about your business?
Consider what is unique about your business. Is it:

- **Your location** – are you the only house clearance service in a particular area?

- **Delivery** – are you the only laundry which collects, dry cleans and delivers on the same day? Do you offer free delivery?

- **Specialist** – do you provide a cleaning service exclusively for ex-military personnel?

- **Flexibility** – are you the only computer trainer who will work on a Saturday?

- **Guarantees** – do you offer a longer guarantee than others in the same business?

- **Range of goods** – do you have the largest selection of golfing accessories in the North East?

- **Quality of goods** – is your furniture handmade, hand carved, hand finished?

- **Customer service** – do you offer exceptional customer service?

- **Pricing** – are your prices lower than your competitors'; inclusive of delivery or one year's servicing?

There is something unique about you or your business: find it and use it.

What are you really selling?
What are you selling or thinking of selling? The answer to this question is vital, because you might believe you're selling something quite different from what your customers are buying. Most of all, people want security, to look good, feel good, be healthy, be valued. When Mrs Smith purchases a car she's not buying a car, she's buying a status symbol, safe transport for her children, independence, freedom, hassle-free motoring or mobility. When Mr Smith buys insurance, he doesn't buy a policy, he buys peace of mind, protection for him and his family. You might offer secretarial

services, but the consultant buys relief from a heavy workload, a more professional image, higher status amongst his colleagues, a more efficient business and increased profits.

Above all you need to be a solution provider.

* How does your product benefit others?
* How does your service improve people's lives?

Consider what people want and provide it – profitably!

Can you specialise?

Many businesses flourish because they specialise or find what's commonly called a niche market. If you're a public relations consultant, for example, this may mean offering your services to football players only. Or if you develop computer software you might specialise in database packages dedicated to food stores. In doing this you may think you're leaving a large market untapped, but in reality it doesn't work that way. What it does mean is that you are addressing the *specific* challenges faced by a *specific* group of people. Your name becomes linked with providing a particular service or product that is perfect for a particular section of society – a niche market.

WHO IS YOUR CUSTOMER?

There are very few products that will appeal to everyone. There is a group of people who will be more inclined than any other to buy what you have to offer, so you need to find out who these potential customers are and focus your attention directly on them.

Your ideal customers

Some products make it easier for you to identify your typical customer. If you produce cosmetics specifically for young teenage girls or an accounting package specifically for car dealers, labelling your ideal customers will be easier.

When building up a profile of your ideal customer, you might include:

* their age
* their sex
* where they live

- their average income
- which newspapers and magazines they read most
- which radio station they listen to most
- which TV station they watch most.

Depending on your product or service you may need to establish other criteria, including:

- their average mortgage
- number of children, if any
- whether their children attend private or state schools
- number of cars per household
- how often they change their car
- whether they holiday abroad, if so where and how often.

If you're unable to find the answers to your questions, you'll have to best guess them. You could do this as a brainstorming session with people whose judgement you value.

If you have existing customers, labelling your typical customer will be easier. By checking who has bought from you in the past you will discover which people buy from you most. Break this down into a profile which includes average age and other criteria and then produce marketing material with this person in mind.

It's worth noting, however, that your current typical customer can change. One massage company found that their average customer was a 35-year-old male manual worker, with an average income of £18,000 per annum visiting an average of once every two months to gain relief from an aching neck and back. By altering the emphasis of their marketing from health only, to health and beauty, the massage company increased their turnover by 250%. Now their typical customer is a 43-year-old female, with an annual income of £30,000, visiting an average of three times every month, and spending more per visit.

GATHERING CUSTOMER INFORMATION

Because your customers are so vital to your overall success, it makes sense to learn all you can about them and what they want. Sending out a questionnaire or survey is often a great way to find out more about potential and existing customers and a very useful way to gather information, provided you've made response easy and, in some instances, offered an incentive to reply.

If you're developing a product which you think would benefit manufacturing companies, for instance, find out who in a particular company would make the decision to buy and call them and/or send a questionnaire. Say you've developed a fact sheet/questionnaire and would value their opinion about your product or service. Be candid, develop rapport and say you'd welcome honest feedback.

The questionnaire needs to be carefully thought out, and preferably no more than two sides of A4 initially. Include a fact sheet about your new product or service and list benefits first, followed by a brief overview of features. Your recipient won't have time to write out every answer, so give them carefully thought out options with tick boxes alongside and space for their own comments. Put their name, position and contact details on there too so they don't have to spend time filling in details. Make it easy for them to return the form – either via a fax, or enclose a self-addressed envelope.

Feedback

You may, of course, get negative feedback, and it's imperative you listen to this. Assess the validity of the comments. Perhaps you overlooked something, or someone has already cornered the market. Maybe your costs are too high or too low. If everyone else is selling the same piece of equipment for around £5,000 and you're offering the same product for £1,000, you may not be taken seriously.

From your feedback you now have the name and contact details of someone who is a potential purchaser of your product. Better than that, you've already made contact, so when you approach them again, they will at least have heard of you. And if you've asked the right questions, you will also have details of how your product will fit into their operations, so you can tailor your marketing material accordingly.

You may feel uneasy about asking others to comment on your business in this way. Maybe you think someone else will use your ideas. It's unlikely – millions of people have hundreds of ideas daily, but very few act upon them. Besides, successful business people know it doesn't pay to adopt an everyone-is-out-to-get-me attitude. Instead:

- focus on your customers

- choose to deal with people you intuitively feel good about

- conduct all your business with integrity

- offer an excellent product or service
- get your marketing right

and your rewards will be great.

Once you sell to someone you can begin to build up details of them and their buying habits. Which marketing method or methods did they respond to? What do they buy? How frequently? What preferences do they have? When did they last buy from you? Do they respond to special offers?

CHOOSING MARKETING METHODS

The marketing methods you choose will depend on a variety of factors: the time and budget you have available; the product or service you're marketing, and your approach to marketing – do you love it or loath it? One thing is certain, when you have an excellent product or service, marketing is much easier. *After all, you're not selling – you're connecting your product with people who want to buy it and that's an extremely valuable service.*

Imagine you sell beds. Out there is someone who recognises that they'll spend around a third of their life in bed, asleep. They've decided to buy a good night's sleep, better health, and a greater sense of well-being (in the form of a bed). By putting your product before them in the shape of a sales letter, advertisement or television commercial, you're giving them the opportunity to have what they want. In marketing your products, you're providing a valuable service by making people aware of what is available to them, in what shape, colour, form, and by making it as easy for them to obtain as possible. Maybe you offer credit terms, no deposit, 0% finance, instant delivery or free bed linen with every order. Whatever it is, they deserve to know so they can make an informed choice. You may include delivery with your goods, which makes your product £25 less expensive overall than your nearest competitor. So your marketing can help save people money – and they'll be glad you did.

Focus on coverage

Throughout this book you will be exposed to a variety of marketing methods. Some will be more appropriate for you than others, but invariably your efforts will include one or more of the following:

- Sales letters
- Direct mail
- Newspaper adverts (display and classified in national, regional and local press)
- Magazine advertisements (general, specialist, business and trade)
- Newsletters
- Radio and TV commercials
- Word of mouth
- Internet
- Advertorials (adverts in newspapers and magazines that look and read like editorial)
- Press releases
- Poster advertising (on underground stations, on buses, billboards at other key sites)
- Leaflets (to be put up in public areas, maybe with a tear-off coupon at the bottom)
- Inserts (flyers inserted loosely or stitched into magazines)
- Point-of-sale displays
- Company or product information brochures.

Every one of the above forms of advertising has things for and against it depending on what you're selling, and the merits of each have to be assessed according to your other research and budget. If you decide that your typical customer is an 18-year-old male music lover you wouldn't place adverts in a retirement magazine, but you might consider advertising in the popular music press and putting dynamic posters on high-profile sites.

You also need to network with people, to draw attention to yourself and your products and services by making yourself available to a much wider group of people. A lot of business is done between people who know or know of each other. It does not mean you get the sale regardless of whether your service is good or not, because this isn't so. It simply means that six months to a year away when someone mentions they need to set up a regular monthly delivery of sculptures to Glasgow, your contact will say, 'I know just the person!'

Many people say that it's not what you know, but who you know that puts you ahead in business, but that's only partly true. Knowing people is essential, but if your product or service is poor, people will soon get to know that too.

Selling abroad

If you have a product or service which you intend to market abroad, you need to consider other factors when producing marketing material. It's not enough simply to write material and have it translated. Direct word-for-word translations can mean something entirely different, and there are cultural differences too. This certainly applies when trading with countries such as Japan, Russia and the USA, and also in Europe which is made up of many different backgrounds and cultures. Similarly, it's unwise to produce the same promotional material for worldwide or even European audiences, and you do need to make yourself aware of the legal requirements each country has regarding marketing.

We often use the word *free* in UK advertising, but this is considered misleading by the French advertising authority who will take you to court if you use it in your advertising. In Germany you cannot issue coupons for a discount off a customer's next purchase, and whilst here in the UK you could promote your product as being better than your competitors' (providing you can prove it), it's not allowed in Scandinavian countries.

> **The best advice is to *take advice* before preparing any marketing materials for use abroad, even with English-speaking countries such as the USA, as there are cultural as well as language differences.**

STAYING AHEAD

Many businesses fail because they don't continually market their business in one form or another. If you neglect the marketing side of your business because you believe you've got enough customers or contracts for the moment, you're making the mistake many failed businesses have made. If you lost your current clients, for whatever reason, where would that leave you? Imagine the time lapse between marketing your services, people responding, making the sale, and actually receiving the money for the job. Could you survive that long? Besides, not every potential customer will become an actual customer on the basis of one advertisement. They may need to see and hear what you're offering many times over before giving you their business.

Is your business growing?

Getting more business is essential because if your business isn't growing it must be in decline, as nothing stays the same however much we may want it to. A competitor can appear at any time and start taking better care of your customers, giving better discounts, better offers and better products, or simply using more effective marketing techniques.

Many people ask, 'What's the point of advertising when my books are already full? I'll only have to turn people down'. In theory yes, but there's nothing wrong with making a virtue of the fact that you don't have space for anyone – at the moment. Explain that you have a waiting list and offer to add their name with no obligation. People like to deal with successful people. Perhaps you run a complementary therapy clinic. Surely it's better to have people waiting to replace those who move away, cancel appointments or take their business elsewhere. If you provide services for the staff of a large organisation and the organisation makes cuts, you lose a large chunk of your business. Besides, people like to think there's a degree of exclusivity about what they do. Belonging to a private health club with a waiting list of potential members holds a great appeal for many people.

You might consider expanding your business, but if particular services can only be provided by you, personally, then you must charge accordingly if demand increases. Alternatively look at delivering your services in a different way if suitable – via a video programme perhaps. *Don't undervalue yourself and what you do.*

Don't be complacent and think you don't need to market. It's a bit like unhitching horses from the front of a moving wagon – initially the wagon will appear to race along at the same speed, but gradually it will get slower and slower, until eventually it grinds to a complete standstill. Stop marketing your business and exactly the same thing can happen to you.

One small engineering company had been run by the same family for over 50 years, and four of the seven staff had spent all their working lives there. Brian, the owner, didn't believe in marketing.

'We've always done alright,' Brian would tell the accountant every time he raised the subject, 'we've got plenty of work, and we've never had to go touting for it.'

But times had changed. Two of the large vehicle repair businesses that relied upon the company were feeling the pinch financially, as fewer customers drove vehicles which needed customised repairs. Failing to recognise the trends, both companies closed within two months of each other, causing Brian to lose 70 per cent of his business. Brian knew he had to do something rapidly, and, finally taking his accountant's advice, he took stock of his business and began a marketing campaign. Without the help of his astute accountant and sympathetic bank manager there is no doubt Brian would have lost his business. As it was, he had to make four of his longest serving staff redundant and reinvest in new equipment. His plan to retire early has been thwarted and at 61 he's working harder than ever. The difference is that he now has a clear marketing strategy in place with other systems to ensure he has a thriving business to sell when he does eventually retire.

KEY POINTS

- Offer an excellent product or service.

- Focus on your customers.

- Provide solutions for people – improve their lives.

- Specialise whenever possible.

- Find ways of doing repeat business.

- Become great at marketing.

- Continue to market – even when order books are full.

2

Advertising – Where and What's Best?

The way you choose to advertise will depend on many things, including: what you're trying to sell; whether it appeals to people locally, nationally or internationally, and your budget. Before you can select where, when and how to advertise, you need to set out what it is you want to achieve. It could be said that whatever you want to achieve – whether it's to promote your services, raise people's awareness, retain your current market share or inform – ultimately your aim is to sell, at some stage, something to someone.

WHAT ARE YOUR OPTIONS?

All businesses need to spend wisely when it comes to marketing, and small businesses especially. Unlike larger organisations, they might not have the necessary cash flow or resources to readvertise should their initial attempts draw a disappointing response.

This chapter focuses on print advertisements, but does offer a snapshot of TV and radio advertising. If there isn't a publication or medium which reaches your chosen market, don't waste money advertising in this way. If you're competing against much larger companies, consider a more direct, more personal approach to your potential customers. That's because if you both run adverts, your competitor will be able to run bigger and better ads, and more frequently.

All new advertisements are experiments, and what works for others may not work for you, but with the benefit of hindsight it's possible to see how some approaches stand a better chance of working and these are outlined in this chapter. Don't spend all your budget on one approach – divide your budget, try several ways and see which work best. In most instances, people need to hear or see what you're offering many times, so to get the most from your advertising, repeat adverts. And remember, whichever advertising options you choose, keep up the momentum, don't just advertise and sit back. Use some of the other methods outlined in this book to back up your advertising campaign and increase your chances of success.

Print advertisements

Look in directories such as *Willings Press Guide* and you will get some idea of the vast number of publications you can advertise in – everything from local to worldwide publications. Because of the specialist nature of many of these it is possible for you to reach a highly targeted group of people.

Newspapers

Advertising in newspapers allows you to reach a large proportion of consumers in a given area and from different social backgrounds. Retailers use this medium as it works well for them, but it wouldn't be so effective for companies who sell products or services to other businesses. Local papers are also useful to sell locally provided products or services, such as beauticians, electricians and gardeners.

Most newspapers have a classified advertisement section, which are simply lines of words under different headings, although many classified sections include boxed adverts known as classified display.

Directories

Yellow Pages, *Thompson* and *Dentons* are examples of national and local directories where there are alphabetical listings of a wide range of goods and services. When people pick up a directory they are actively seeking a product or service, and around 75 per cent of them will make a call to an advertiser. But that doesn't mean they will necessarily call the person they were looking for initially. Their eye may be taken by a bigger or better ad, or someone who highlights their specific problem. These sorts of advertisements can work well for businesses such as Interflora florists, drain clearance, plumbers, removals and house clearance services, but not for professions such as packaging consultants or journalists. Because there is no editorial content as such in a directory, people turn to them for a reason, not to browse for something new. Be careful about putting time-sensitive material in a directory as it might have a life span of a year or more, so things like prices, offers and delivery may alter.

- As long as you are running your own business (or are self-employed) and have a land-line telephone, you are entitled to a free listing in *Yellow Pages*. You can have a one-line entry under an existing heading of your choice and you must include your full address. Call 0800 533 433 for further details or to book your entry.

Trade directories
Most industries and professions have their own trade directories and journals. These are geared towards specialist markets, such as packaging (corrugated packaging perhaps), plastics and nursing, which would suit businesses geared towards a specialist market.

Magazines
There are magazines specifically targeted to most groups of consumers, but they are more expensive to advertise in than local newspapers. It is rare for small local businesses to advertise in popular weekly magazines as advertising can be expensive and would reach more people outside their area than within it. Magazines are less frequent than newspapers, but are kept and referred to for longer. Some of the monthly glossy magazines do feature classified-style ads towards the rear of their publications which can prove cost effective for some small businesses to advertise in.

Notice-boards
You can use notice-boards in hospitals, supermarkets, libraries, launderettes and newsagents if this is where you think your potential customers will look. You can put up cards, or a poster with tear-off slips at the bottom (usually with your contact number, or money-off incentives). This allows readers to take your details even if they haven't got a pen with them, and stops them removing the whole flyer from the board. If you offer a word-processing service, for example, consider putting a flyer with tear-off strips in a prominent position on a university campus. Many students are happy to pay someone else to produce an error-free essay or dissertation rather than struggle along with it themselves.

Inserts
These are leaflets or brochures which you print and newspapers and magazines put inside their publications at a cost per thousand. Depending on the size of the magazine, you will probably need to print a minimum of 10,000. Some magazines limit the number of inserts they take, others don't. Negotiate to be the first (or top) insert as effectiveness can diminish the more there are.

Radio

Local radio stations can have more listeners than national radio. In west Dorset, for instance, Radio 2 trails into second place behind Wessex FM. This local station reaches an average of 57,000 adults per month, which is 50 per cent of the population. The majority of the station's listeners are aged between 35 and 44, divided almost equally between the sexes, and as such are likely to be interested in purchasing products such as cars, windows, DIY materials, holidays and mortgages. As a large percentage of listeners have children, advertisements targeting families can also be worthwhile. One museum increased its turnover by 110 per cent after a series of advertisements.

Many local stations offer special packages for first-time advertisers, so contact your local station to see whether they do. Wessex FM, for instance, offers a one-off proposal for first-time advertisers which involves a standard 30-second commercial (produced by the Commercial Production Department). This is played four times every day (except Friday and Saturday) for four weeks, giving a total of 80 commercials which will be heard by 39,000 of their listeners an average of almost seven times.

Television

Advertising rates on national television will probably be prohibitive for the small business, but at some stage the cost of advertising on independent local or cable TV may be an option.

Advertising on Westcountry Television, for example, allows advertisers to reach 90 per cent of the area's 1.6 million resident population. The cost depends on three factors:

- length of advertisement
- when it's shown
- how often it's shown.

Westcountry offers free help and advice on planning, and in some cases might even help you fund the cost of making your commercial. Many businesses have run successful campaigns including garden centres, fabric shops, pet food suppliers and travel agents.

On some cable stations it may be possible to buy time during someone else's show. Try to find a link – if someone is running a DIY show, for instance, perhaps you could buy time to promote your equipment-hire service.

WHAT TO EXPECT FOR YOUR MONEY

When you ring a newspaper or other advertising medium about placing an advertisement they will invariably send you a rate card. This rate card carries details of the types of advertisements available.

Classifieds
Usual options include private and trade lineage (classifieds), display and semi display.

In the case of lineage, you pay a set cost per word, and an extra sum per word if you want it printed in bold. You can choose to have a line above and below at additional cost, or have it put in a box. The set up does vary slightly from publication to publication, but many now offer a classified display which is charged per single column centimetre. If a newspaper charges £6 per single column centimetre, and you book a display box 10 cm deep and two columns wide, the advert will cost you £120. Most publications give a series discount which reduces the overall price per advert if you book a certain number of adverts.

Box numbers
Some people choose to use a box number on their advertisements and collect their responses from the newspaper's offices or have them redirected. The cost of box numbers varies but a fee of around £25 is charged by many regional newspapers. Be aware, however, that newspaper box numbers in adverts can significantly reduce response.

Run of paper
The run of paper refers to the rest of the paper apart from the classifieds. Adverts here are charged per column centimetre and usual options are:

- the title corner (small set size advert on masthead next to publication's name)
- front page solus (only advertisement on front page amid editorial)
- back page solus (only advertisement on back page amid editorial)
- full, half or quarter page.

Additional charges are made for:

- specifying on which page you want your ad to appear

- taking an *unspecified* right-hand page (a right-hand page is a better position)

- spot or full colour if it's an option.

Many advertisers never pay the rates shown on a rate card and you should be aware of this. If you are selling products by mail order, for example, the newspaper or magazine you're considering advertising with will do very well to have you as a customer. For this reason, there's nothing wrong with asking what their mail order discount is.

Alternatively, ask them about *distress* space. This is space left over when the newspaper's deadline is imminent. Rather than have wasted or unsold space they sometimes repeat an advertisement which ran in a previous issue, which they don't charge the advertiser for. If you do get *distress* space, you won't normally have a say about where your ad is placed, but for the small business, getting advertising space at such reduced rates can make it worthwhile. You can save as much as 50 per cent when buying distress space – and one publisher is said to have bought advertising space at less than 10 per cent of the rate card price.

You could also ask about paying *per enquiry*. In some instances you might be able to convince the decision-maker about making payment per enquiry received as a result of your advertisement.

Using a media agent

Many people can secure their own discounts when buying advertising space, but if you've been unable to, or the thought of haggling fills you with dread, consider using a media buyer. Buyers receive a commission from the people they buy space or time from, so you pay them nothing. If your advertising budget is really low or you are only buying distress space, the percentage fees they receive from the media will also be extremely low. In this case the buyer might not consider it worth their while. However, many recognise that if they help small businesses obtain good advertising deals when they're starting out, those same companies will grow and turn into big clients.

Is circulation everything?

If you're considering placing adverts in several publications, ask for media packs from each. These packs include rate cards and circulation and readership figures. If a readership profile isn't included, ask for one, as this provides a breakdown of the socio-economic status, occupations, demographic location and interests of the readership. Imagine you're considering advertising your art video in two magazines – *Specialist Art One* and *Specialist Art Two*. Both are monthly magazines and appear to be aimed at the same specialist audience. *Specialist Art One* has a readership of 100,000 and *Specialist Art Two* has a readership of 75,000. Initially you may opt for advertising with *Specialist Art One*, but when scrutinising the readership profile of both you realise that whilst *Specialist Art One* has a higher readership, it attracts a much higher percentage of mature, experienced artists. *Specialist Art Two*, however, attracts almost all art students and novices, the ideal audience for your video.

SELLING DIRECT FROM THE PAGE

Selling direct from the page means just that. You place an advertisement about your product in a publication and people respond by ordering. You'll find countless examples in national, regional and specialist newspapers and magazines. The advert tells you about the product (and might show photographs or graphics), gives the price, and leads you through the ordering process. Readers are asked to order in one of several ways, including:

- telephone, quoting a credit card number
- completing and posting a coupon (possibly freepost), complete with cheque
- writing a short note, together with a cheque, asking for goods to be sent
- faxing through an order form or letter, complete with credit card number.

Response

A major benefit of selling direct from the page is that, depending on the publication you advertise in, your response will be reasonably quick. In a daily newspaper, half or more of your responses will arrive in the first three to five days. For weekly publications, half or more will appear in around six to eight days of the first response, and for monthly magazines half or more will arrive within three weeks of your first response. These are guidelines only, as obviously much depends on the strength of your product, offer and advertisement. And unless you say otherwise, every order will arrive with money! If you ask for the money with the order it helps you avoid cash flow problems. Simply reassure the reader that if they're not absolutely delighted, they can have their money back by return – guaranteed.

Mail Order Protection Scheme (MOPS)

You have probably noticed that many advertisements carry the Mail Order Protection Scheme logo. When people respond to advertisements displaying the MOPS logo they know that should the ordered goods fail to arrive as a result of an advertiser going bankrupt or ceasing to trade they will have their money returned to them. Mail order advertisers join MOPS by paying fees, which vary according to how much they spend on advertising. (See Useful Addresses.) There are some national newspapers which insist on their mail order advertisers being MOPS members.

Classified adverts

Classified advertisements are often the major source of revenue for newspapers up and down the country. People turn to classifieds because they want to buy, which can make this a very useful place for you to advertise. It's also one of the cheapest ways to get your advertisements read. Because classified advertisements are all about selling, you need to be specific about what it is you're offering – no preamble, no setting the scene, just straight-to-the-point advertising. Although classified sections have trade headings, most advertisements appear in the long line of ads which people scan.

Make sure the first words you use in your advertisement make the reader stop to see what you have to offer. *Free* is always a good opener, as are *discount, guarantee, make money, secure.* For example, *Free Gold Style Frame with every Times Square, Empire State Building, Twin Towers or Broadway poster purchased...*

Classified ads need to be punchy and grab the reader immediately, so don't bother with subtleties or weak words such as *possibly, maybe* or *can often* – use *definitely, will* or *always*, providing they're truthful of course. Sometimes a cheaper classified advert will draw a better response than a larger display ad if the latter is in a poor position.

If you have more than one product or service to offer, take out advertisements for each to avoid diluting the impact of each advert. Look at the classified advertisements yourself and see which adverts stand out to you. What words are they using? Do they have the first few words in bold? Is the advert boxed? Is it effective? You could always call a couple of the regular advertisers and ask if they're happy with their response rate. Do your competitors advertise here on a regular basis? If so, it may be an indication of how good a place it is for you to advertise.

An advertisement in the classified section of a newspaper will not work well for every type of business. If you are a training or management consultant, vet, counsellor, interior designer or dentist, for example, most people wouldn't consider looking in the classified section of a local newspaper for these sorts of services. Many national and specialist glossy magazines now have a classified section which may be more suitable. A dentist offering a revolutionary teeth-whitening product might find an advert in a beauty magazine could work well.

GUARANTEED TO WHITEN TEETH INSTANTLY
Revolutionary new toothpaste developed by leading dentist
Available only by mail order
£9.99 including p&p buys you two months' supply
Make cheques payable to Dazzle and send to ...Today!

As a general rule, classified advertisements sell lower price products than display.

Display adverts

The size of the advertisement will determine how much you can say but, as this is your only chance to make the sale, ensure every piece of information the reader needs is included. If you can afford a full-page display advertisement you will have lots of room to list benefits, features, guarantees and ordering details. Most of these type of ads carry a coupon which the purchaser fills in and returns. In this instance always put your address and telephone number elsewhere in the advert too. This means that if another reader wants to order, they still can, even if the original coupon has been cut out.

If your budget won't run to such a large advert, don't worry. There's nothing quite like a small budget to concentrate the mind. When you ring to enquire about advertising, never write an advert over the phone. Adverts need to be carefully thought out, so don't be pushed into coming up with something quickly. Above all, your adverts need to be effective, so let creativity take a back seat, and consider how you're going to push the reader into action.

A display advertisement (if correctly written) will attract people who weren't necessarily thinking of buying your product, but who are drawn to it when they see your advert amongst the editorial. Remember, the earlier in the paper your advert appears the better – after all, the main news starts off at the front. A right-hand page is preferable too, and if your ad contains a coupon, ensure it's on the outer edge of the page to make it easier to cut out.

SELLING VIA THE TWO-STEP PROCESS

The two-step process entails writing an advertisement, commercial or sales letter which gets people to send for more information. This is a less risky way of marketing as you're getting people to declare their interest in your product or service without asking them to buy. This allows you to gather names and addresses of prospects you can then target.

Many advertisements produce enquiries, even those intended to sell direct from the page. That's because the reader has thought of a point which hasn't been covered, or they need further reassurance.

If you're offering a home study course on interior design, consider preparing an information booklet which shows how people can transform their homes, impress others with their design skills and possibly start their own business. Your advertisement wouldn't ask people to send for the course, but for a **free** fully detailed booklet entitled *Interior Design – Home Study Course...* Now all the reader has to do is send or ring their details through, which, as there's no risk involved, they're more likely to do. By creating awareness and knowledge of what you offer you collect the names and addresses of people who are genuinely interested in your product or service. Eventually with additional marketing you can turn these prospects into customers, by converting their interest into actual sales.

One company wanted to attract a list of people interested in their business books so they advertised on the front page of a daily national newspaper, selling a business report. The cost of the advert was covered by the number of reports sold, but the company ended up with something even more useful – the names and addresses of people interested in buying written business information.

If you sell via the two-step process, you don't yet have to be a member of MOPS to advertise in those publications who insist on it for direct sale advertisements.

Much depends on the product you're trying to sell, your budget and whether you're trying to sell it direct from the page or through the two-step process. Many marketers have different thoughts on this. Some advise using small display ads rather than classifieds if your budget is limited. This is because display ads appear before classifieds and will attract the reader who wasn't necessarily looking to buy but sees the ad amongst editorial. Advocates of classified advertising maintain that people looking in the classified section are actively looking to purchase. Only you can decide whether your product or service is something that people will actively seek in this way. As always you need to be objective and put yourself in your prospect's shoes.

ADVERTISING BEFORE PRODUCTION

There are some instances when you might consider advertising a product or service before it's available. This gives you the added benefit of being able to gauge response before you go to the expense of producing or buying it.

If you have knowledge of how a particular part of industry works, for example, you could consider selling that knowledge. Your calculations show that your specialist expertise could save medium-sized food manufacturers between £10,000 and £25,000 per year on their production and distribution costs. As a consultant you may charge £500 per day to work with companies helping them to do this. On this basis your income is limited to the number of days you can work with each company, which means you will reach a limited audience and your income will reach a ceiling too.

However, if you produce the information in a format which companies can use themselves, you will be able to reach a far wider audience and leave yourself free to act in a consultancy capacity with clients of your choice. You might consider producing the information as a 700-page report, or on CD ROM, and include a comprehensive illustrated step-by-step guide, suppliers' lists and other specialist information. If you feel unsure about how the report would sell and how much you could sell it for, this would be a good item to advertise prior to production. You could:

1. Advertise a special pre-production offer. This is where you advertise the package as being available from a certain future date and offer readers a special lower pre-production price if they

order their copy now. If for instance your report is to sell at £750, you could offer it for £570; *or*

2. Advertise at the normal price and show delivery as being within 28 days.

In the first example, ordering doesn't have to mean paying with order. If the production date is too far ahead, people may be reluctant to do so unless you guarantee not to cash their cheques until their order is due to be released. Alternatively you can invoice them prior to publication.

It can be difficult to gauge how long a project will take to complete, so err on the side of caution, as you must be certain you can deliver on time. Once the report is finished and in production (in whatever form) you can then reduce delivery times as appropriate.

There is nothing like a full order book to concentrate the mind, so this is often a great way to get a project off the ground, and less risky than producing first, selling second. When producing your initial adverts you must concentrate on the benefits to potential customers. If the response is good, you will design your package around customer response.

KEY POINTS

- Set a firm objective and consider all options.
- Advertising rates are always negotiable.
- Check the readership profiles of your chosen media.
- Selling direct from the page draws a quicker response.
- Two-step selling is less risky.

3

Make Good Adverts Great

Every day we are bombarded with advertisements in one form or another – on the television and radio; in magazines and newspapers; and on posters, packaging and leaflets that come through our door. How much of it do you read, if any?

When a sales representative of a local newspaper rings the local hardware store to see if they'd like to place an advert, the conversation often ends like this:

Customer: 'Well, we've never had much response before, if any, from the ads we've placed with you.'
Sales rep: 'I'm surprised to hear that? Do you ask your customers how they heard about you?'
Customer: 'Well, er, no, not really, but most of them have been customers for years.'
Sales rep: 'But our current promotion is featuring shops in your vicinity to promote trade in the area, it would be a shame to be left out.'
Customer: 'I suppose so...Oh all right then, book me the smallest set space.'
Sales rep: 'What would you like me to put in your advertisement?'
Customer: 'I'll send you a copy of my business card, put that in, that's what I did before.'
Sales rep: 'Thank you.'

Many small businesses simply reproduce their business cards or similar details in advertisements, which is a great way of ensuring the advert gets *overlooked*.

BE BELIEVABLE

Before you write an advertisement you need to establish what benefits your product gives to the end user. You can start by examining the features of your product – such as its size, location and capacity. If you're selling swimming pools, for example, one feature may be an inbuilt self-cleaning filter. You'll find it useful to list features as a way of helping you determine what the true benefits of your product or service are. Benefits of self-cleaning swimming pool filters include: you always have clean water (much healthier); you don't have the hassle of remembering to change it (peace of mind); you don't need to use a pool cleaning service (saves money); and you don't have to devote so much time to pool maintenance (so you save time too). By arranging the benefits in order of importance you can arrive at a major benefit and use it in your headline.

Imagine you're writing an advertisement to sell bicycles. Do people buy bicycles? No, they buy ways to entertain themselves, to travel, as gifts and to get fit. So buying a bicycle is an opportunity to:

- get fit
- look healthier
- travel
- care for the environment
- occupy children.

These are just some of the benefits, which in turn can:

- give enormous pleasure (seeing your children and yourself enjoy the outdoor life)

- improve your outlook on life (a healthy body equals a healthy mind)

- allow you to set a good example (to your family, peers and community).

These are some of the benefits of buying a bicycle which you need to convey to your prospect. So examine your product or service carefully to determine what the real benefits are, because that's what you're selling.

To avoid confusing the *benefits* of a product or service with its *features*, consider the following: if the cycle has puncture-proof tyres, that's a feature of the bicycle. The benefit of this is that when you or your children are out riding there's no risk of a puncture so you can ride with confidence and feel safer. You and your children have peace of mind.

Unique Selling Proposition (USP)

Everything has a **USP**. This is something about you, your product or service which is unique. Something which is different from your competitors. Look at your competitors' advertisements and see what they don't say. Capitalise on your uniqueness and think of ways you can weave this credibly into your advertisement.

Credibility building

If you produce an advertising video or commercial, demonstrations should show how easy your product is to use, how it outperforms its closest rival (as long as it does) and how efficient it is at doing all you say it can do.

In all forms of advertising, testimonials from highly satisfied clients are a great way of showing how your service genuinely benefits others. Or you can show before and after pictures to illustrate how your product really does deliver all you say it can.

Highlight the advantages your product or service offers. Is your valeting service quicker, your toolmaking more accurate? Are your contract prices lower? Do you deal with specialist projects, and is your cleaning service more efficient? Use positive language to show how, with your product or service, the buyer can achieve their desired outcome.

Some products can be marketed negatively. By showing someone with bad body odour being avoided by friends and colleagues you can spur them into buying your revolutionary body spray. The product itself isn't appealing, but what it does is.

Body copy

Body copy is the name given to the main body of wording that comes after the headline (which is dealt with later in this chapter) and it must not only *be true*, it must *sound true*. To break up the bulk of the body copy you need to put plenty of subheadings in to act as signposts to the reader. Write subheadings such as: *Send No Money Now* or *Many Have Found Complete Relief* or *Join Today,* anything which breaks up the long tracts of text and urges the reader forward.

In some newspapers or magazines you can produce your advertisement to look the same as the editorial. If the newspaper uses a particular typeface, use this in the same size, and spread it across three columns (or however many columns the publication uses). This is often referred to as an advertorial, and in many publications the word advertorial or advertisement is written in small letters across the top, although some publications may leave the word out.

Photographs
A photo in an advertisement improves response if it's relevant. You can build credibility by using real people, products and examples. Put people in your photos if possible, and have them smile and look friendly. Head-and-shoulder shots work better than full-body pictures unless you're showing something where it would be relevant to show the whole body. Because the photograph and the headline are looked at within seconds, there should be a connection between the two. *Always give a photo a caption.*

GET ATTENTION

Your headline must have immediate impact if it's to work. Its job is to get attention and you can do this only by appealing to the reader's self-interest. So many small businesses simply put who they are, where they are, and how to get in touch. For example:

Bryant's Hardware
XYZ Street
Any Town
Tel: 000 Mobile: 000

This is not a good advertisement. This doesn't answer the 'What use is this to me?' question that people automatically ask.
   A good headline:

- attracts the reader's attention
- expresses the most important benefit
- can be long, rather than short
- appeals to the type of people you want to attract
- compels people to read further
- will improve response dramatically.

You need to touch people's emotions and their lives and make them want to know more.

> **The whole purpose of your advert is to make someone act.**
> **And the only way you can do this is by making people stop**
> **and read what you have to say.**

Imagine the above hardware store is in an area concerned about its drinking water. The hardware store stocks a revolutionary jug water filter which is guaranteed to remove the impurities from the local water supply, so they advertise. Consider the following two headlines:

1. *BRYANT'S HARDWARE*

2. *'Here's How To Have Safe Drinking Water For Your Family, Peace Of Mind For You...'*

The first draws a 'So what?' response, and the second touches your emotions. Using the second headline in their local paper would make readers want to know more.

When writing headlines use a capital letter at the beginning of all words, as it can make it much easier to read:

Use Upper Case And Lower Case Letters Like This
In A Headline

DO NOT USE ALL CAPITAL LETTERS IN A
HEADLINE LIKE THIS

Notice it is more difficult to read the second example. Your aim is always to make it as easy as possible for your reader.

Put inverted commas around your headline too, as in:

'Now I Can Talk About Stocks and Shares with the Rest Of Them'

The following are just some of the words and phrases which have been proved over and over again to work well in headlines. You can adapt the examples shown to suit what you're offering.

- **How to...**
  How To Get Rid Of Tax Worries for Good
  How To Stop That Embarrassing Blushing
  How To Feel In The Mood – Whatever Your Age!

- **Here's A...**
  Here's A Great Way To Write For Money
  Here's A Quick And Easy Way To Be Blonde
  Here's A Short Cut Accountants Don't Tell You

- **To A...**
  To A Woman Who Wants More From Her Partner
  To A Man Who's About To Retire
  To A Father Whose Son Is 16

- **How I...**
  How I Improved My Spelling In One Evening
  How I Made A Million From A Simple Idea
  How I Retired 15 Years Early – With No Loss Of Income!

- **Do You...**
  Do You Want To Forget The Past And Start A New Life?
  Do You Want To Learn To Swim In Three Days?
  Do You Want To Look Bronzed and Healthy All Year Round?

- **Free...**
  Free Report – *How To Raise Successful Kids*
  Free To Sole Traders – £7 to others
  Free Book Reveals The Secrets of Self-Made Millionaires

- **At last...**
  At Last, The Truth About Men
  At Last, A Foolproof Way To Make Money
  At Last, The Pain Relief You've Been Waiting For

- **To...**
  To Parents Who Want To Raise Happy Children
  To People Who Want To Be Their Own Boss
  To People Who Want To Drive A Better Car

A good headline is one which works for you. So important is the headline in your adverts that simply by changing all or part of it you can double and treble the response. There are more ideas for great headlines in Chapter 5, Write Great Sales Letters.

CALL TO ACTION

You need to make your adverts so compelling that people can't resist what you're offering. Even so, some people mean to order, but simply don't get around to it. To avoid this, you could write: *So send in this coupon now to make sure it doesn't slip your mind* or *Post Your*

Free Prize Draw Entry Today! Or *It's vital that you respond immediately if you want to take advantage of the early order discount.*

If you offer a demonstration, you could write: *Call us today on 0800 00 00 00 for a free demonstration in the comfort of your own home* or *Hurry into our showroom for a free demonstration – this half-price offer ends on the 31st of this month* or *Reach for the phone now – if you're one of the first 50 callers you'll get a free keep-fit video whether you buy or not.*

Give people a reason to act today – an incentive, free offer, extra goods, money off, anything which means they act.

When you place an order form in an advertisement you have to make special considerations. If the form is going to be sited in one of the bottom corners of the advert you need to establish whether the advert is going to appear on a right-hand or left-hand page (right is always preferable). This is so you can make sure the form appears on the outside edge of the page. This saves the reader struggling to cut or tear it away from the centre fold. Your job is to make response as easy as possible. Include urgent statements, such as:

Please rush me my copy of...

Yes, I want to be the proud owner of...within 7 hours

For an even faster service, call 00 00 00

Ensure the reader has all the information they want and need to act upon your offer. It's easy to overlook obvious things, such as:

- Is postage and packing free?
- Can payment be made by credit card?
- How soon can you deliver?
- What guarantees are there?

HOW TO WRITE YOUR OWN ADVERTS

It is perfectly possible for you to write (copywrite) your own adverts. That's because copywriting is a skill you can learn. It's about writing which sells, promotes, informs, raises awareness or instructs. You need a reasonable command of the language, but you don't need great literary skills. In becoming an avid reader of other people's copy you'll help yourself even further, especially when you analyse all you read. Ask yourself what messages, words and headlines worked on you, and why. Before you write:

- Always plan – it's essential
- Find out all there is to know about your product or service
- List your product's or service's features
- Turn each of the features into a benefit or benefits
- Find out as much as possible about your target customer
- Look at things from your customer's perspective
- Select the major benefit for your headline
- Determine where your copy is to fit and where it will be seen (brochure, poster, sales letter...)
- Remain objective
- Set yourself a realistic deadline, and stick to it.

Words are everything in marketing. You can make an average advert stand out simply by changing a few words, or turn an unsuccessful advert into a successful one by rephrasing what's on offer. Use emphasis when writing, but don't overdo things or you will accentuate nothing.

Often one of the biggest challenges faced when you write your own copy is to remain objective. When you're close to a product or service, it's easy to become complacent about what you offer and to completely overlook the obvious benefits. Talk to your customers and ask what it is about your product, service or the way you do business that appeals to them.

Help yourself further by reading copywriting books. *Writing Great Copy* reveals the essential techniques professional copywriters use to consistently write words that sell (see Further Reading).

If you really don't have the time or inclination to write your own copy – don't. It will be more cost-effective to hire a copywriter. Often a freelance copywriter will have design, marketing and layout skills which can be an enormous help to the small business. If they don't come recommended, ask to see samples of their work and their previous client list. Above all, trust your instincts. If you feel this is the person who could write you excellent copy, you're probably right.

Remember:

- Push the reader to take immediate action – offer incentives, time limits.

- People are attracted to the word 'free'.

- People focus on a coupon longer if there's a picture on it.

TESTING, TESTING, ONE-TWO-THREE

To gauge where your business comes from you need to keep records. Place source codes on coupons, advertisements and order forms, and get into the habit of asking new customers or enquirers how they heard about you. Armed with this information you will know where your business comes from, and where and how to advertise to get more. Keep records of enquiries separate from sales. This way, for example, you will see that if advert A generates 120 sales and 20 enquiries, and advert B generates 120 enquiries and 20 sales, which advert worked best at generating actual sales.

If you advertise in a daily newspaper you will know far quicker how your advert is working than if you placed it in a directory. But judge from your overall response, not from a section of it, otherwise you won't be looking at the complete picture.

If you decide to run two adverts, you need to test which works best. Change only one element at a time otherwise you won't know which element caused the increase or decrease in response. You could change the headline, subheading, free gift, or any element, but don't forget to record which sales and enquiries were generated from which.

Poor response?

If your response is poor, you need to question many things. Did you advertise on the right day, in the right season, to the right audience? Unless your advert has a compelling reason why people should respond straight away, they might think, 'Oh that's nice' and move on.

Being in the right place at the right time is what you're trying to achieve. So consider where you would look, and when, if you needed the product or service you're offering.

If you find that a product isn't selling as you hoped, don't just assume it's too pricey. Change the niche you've created for it. Often by changing people's perceptions of your product or service, you can actually sell more by putting the price up.

Whatever your response, you need to continue marketing in one form or another. You will eventually see which adverts pull consistently and be able to test elements of that particular ad to increase response even more. As you develop all your promotional activities, your sales will increase as your efforts reinforce one another.

Remember, advertising isn't an exact science. Use all the pointers in this book to give yourself the best chance of getting the right advert before the right person on the right day.

KEY POINTS

- Write headlines which have immediate impact.

- Make adverts easy to read.

- Use source codes to record where *every* response come from.

- Remain objective when writing your own copy.

- Be aware of all the laws that affect you.

- Test adverts by changing one element at a time.

- View adverts as one part of your overall marketing campaign.

4

Create Effective Mailings

Direct mail is one of the fastest growing ways you can advertise yourself and your business. It can be as simple as sending a letter to an existing or potential customer. Or you may choose to include leaflets, brochures or other material, depending on your product, your budget and what you hope to achieve. If your budget is small, you can still achieve a lot with direct mail. Besides, there's nothing like a limited budget for getting you focused.

Before you mail anything, you have to decide what you want to achieve from your mailing. Perhaps you want the reader to:

- order a specific product immediately
- ask for more details of this or other products
- redeem an enclosed voucher within a certain time.

Or maybe you simply want to raise people's awareness about you, your products and services. Whatever it is, you must have a clear goal in mind before you can plan an effective direct mail campaign.

HOW TO SOURCE NAMES

It's important to select carefully the people you send mailshots to. There are several ways in which you can gather names, and in the first instance it is worth checking your own customer records for people who have:

- bought a *similar* product from you before
- bought the *same* product, if it's repeatable
- bought an *associated* product
- *responded* to previous promotions, but not actually bought
- *enquired* about some aspect of your product or service.

The importance of keeping good records is highlighted by the above.

The more of your own names and addresses you can use the better. These are people who are already aware of you and what you offer. The last example, people who have enquired about some aspect of your business, provides you with a valuable lesson in that it is imperative that you take the name and contact details of anyone and everyone who enquires about your products or services. It may well be that what you had to offer didn't fit their requirements at that time – it could be different now.

Because it costs up to six times more to obtain a new customer than to retain one you have already, it makes sense to concentrate your efforts on those you already do business with. A mailshot doesn't have to be just about selling products. You could write to selected customers and send them money-off coupons simply for being such a valued customer, or perhaps it's been a year since they first bought from you. A few well-chosen words really can have a huge positive impact, especially for a small business.

Renting lists
If you don't have a list of existing customers, or you want to target other prospects, you might consider renting or buying a list from a list broker. There are two types of list available in general – consumer and business.

Consumer lists
These target individuals at home and fall into three main groups:

1. **Compiled** – lists compiled specifically for rental from public sources such as share registers and the electoral roll.

2. **Response** – lists generated in response to advertising or direct marketing and including subscribers to magazines, mail order buyers and competition entrants.

3. **Questionnaires** – lists of gathered information about hobbies and interests as well as other general information.

Business lists
These target companies and their employees:

1. **Compiled** – again from public sources such as Companies House and membership lists of trade and professional bodies. They are also researched by telemarketing and can offer selections by categories including company size and industry type.

2. **Response** – can include exhibition attendees, subscription lists, equipment buyers.

List your needs
There are thousands of ready-made lists available, and the Direct Marketing Association (see Useful Addresses) will put you in touch with list brokers who can rent or sell you a list. Before contacting a broker, however, write down some of the details you want from your list. This could include some or all of the following:

For consumer lists
- surname
- title
- first name
- marital status
- address
- telephone number
- age
- sex
- occupation
- income.

The above is just a sample of basic information you will invariably need to know. In addition you may find other criteria useful, depending on what you're selling. Things such as:

- Do they own a caravan?
- Are they keen golfers?
- Do they invest in stocks and shares?
- Are they property owners?
- Number of children, if any, plus their ages.

The possibilities are endless. The more specific you are about the type of people you want to reach, the easier it is for a list broker to help you. It's the same with contacting businesses too. In addition to getting standard information such as:

- contact name
- contact's job title
- company name
- company address
- company telephone number

- company fax number
- company email address
- type of business
- years trading
- number of employees
- annual turnover

if you are selling information technology solutions, for example, your additional criteria may be:

- Do they have their own website or domain?

Lists come in different formats and you need to check that your supplier can provide them in the form you want. The most common are self-adhesive labels or computer disk, but increasingly they are being supplied direct by modem or email.

The direct mail industry, like many others, has its own jargon, such as nett names and goneaways, so ask if you're not certain what something means.

The Direct Mail Association (DMA) produces lists of its members, including list brokers. You can call them on (020) 7321 2525 or visit their website on: *www.dma.org.uk*

Storing customer information

Keeping information is only of use if you can retrieve it quickly and easily when you need it, and that's where computers come in. Not only does database software allow you to call up any customer's details when you need to, depending on what information you hold, you can also select specific customers using certain criteria. If, for example, you have a product which you know will appeal to people over the age of 35, who have an income in excess of £30,000 a year, and children under the age of 12, you could ask the computer to list them. You can send the relevant material to these selections rather than wasting money by mailing everyone on your database.

Consider what information will be useful to you when building a database. Don't just think of what you need now, but of what information will be useful to you in the future. By separating the information into separate fields you make retrieval of specific information easier. You could start with:

- title
- surname

- first name(s)
- full address
- work telephone number
- home telephone number
- age
- children (including ages and sexes)
- annual income
- combined annual income (if with partner or married)
- credit cards
- computer owner.

Include all details of their history with you, whether enquiries or purchases. If enquirers, note which promotion prompted their enquiry, and if they are already customers, include what they bought, when they bought it and in response to which promotion. Note also how they paid. As your relationship with these people grows you can add to the information you hold.

With all information collected, it's vital to ensure it's:

- up to date
- correct.

If you run an industrial cleaning service, for instance, people will be irritated if you write ... *as it's already a year since you used our twilight 'Spring' cleaning service, we thought* ... when in fact you cleaned their carpets just three months ago. They'll believe that if you can get one thing wrong, you can get something else wrong too, and their trust levels can drop.

Keep within the law

If you do store information about living people on computer (or you have such information processed on a computer by others, such as an accountant or computer bureau) you probably need to register under the Data Protection Act 1984. This Act contains laws about compiling and using information about living people and used to apply only to information stored on a computer.

The current Data Protection Act 1998 (due to come into effect early in 2000) has been extended. It now includes information which is recorded as part of a 'relevant filing system' where the records are structured, by reference either to individuals or to criteria relating to individuals, so that specific information relating to a particular individual is readily accessible. This definition will therefore now include some types of manual data. You are advised to check to ensure you are up to date with the current position. You can do this via the Registrar's home page: *http://www.open.gov.uk/dpr/dprhome.htm* or call (01625) 545737.

Alternatively you can write to: The New Law Section, Office of the Data Protection Register, Wycliffe House, Water Lane, Wilmslow, Cheshire SK9 5AF.

The Data Protection Act 1998 – An Introduction highlights the differences between the Data Protection Acts of 1984 and 1998 whilst also providing a broad guide to the 1998 Act as a whole. The initial guide is available from either the Registrar's home page or through the Registrar's office. See also listings under Useful Addresses.

To comply with the Act you need to give people an opportunity to choose not to give you the information you want, and if a customer asks that you stop mailing them you must do so. You may like to put a sentence such as:

> *From time to time we send out promotional material about our products. Please tick this box if you DO NOT want to receive any of this material.*

SENDING OUT

The contents of direct mail packages vary. Invariably, it will always include a letter, and because a letter is such an important part of a mailing, the following chapter is dedicated to creating a successful sales letter. But whether you enclose anything else or not, consider other things first.

The Royal Mail offer a wide range of services and products which can help you send out your direct mail package. These include franking, prepaid envelopes, mailsort and preprinted envelopes.

Brochures

A brochure outlines information about you, your company and services. Some companies provide more than one product or service and produce a brochure for each, but you'd need to gauge the cost-effectiveness of this. In general terms, a brochure tends to be useful for longer where prices, availability and things which are subject to change are omitted from the copy.

Depending on your budget, brochures can be in full colour on glossy paper stock, or if you have a suitable computer and printer you can produce your own in-house. There are companies which provide A4 sheets of card with graphics already printed on them in various designs and colours. These are designed to run through your printer so you can overprint your own information. You then fold them along pre-scored lines to produce an instant brochure. Paper Direct, for example, provide a range of templates and designs to choose from, which allow consultants and small businesses to project a professional image with minimal outlay.

Lift notes

A lift note is often enclosed in direct mail packages... *If you're still undecided, please read this note*... is a common statement to have on the outside of a lift note. It needs to be written on different paper (smaller size and different texture maybe) by someone other than the sender of the sales letter. It could be from another satisfied customer or a well-respected citizen and may say... *Perhaps you think this offer sounds too good to be true, or there's a catch. Let me assure you*... Or... *I'm puzzled why you're not taking advantage of this exciting offer. After all, you've nothing to lose! But maybe there's something that I've missed, so why not drop me a line*...

Outer envelope

When you gather your post in the morning, which letters do you open first? Which ones do you look forward to opening? Probably the ones with handwritten envelopes, because they're likely to be from friends and people you wish to hear from. If you can write your envelopes by hand, do so. Large companies are always trying to create a handwritten look on their envelopes by using various typefaces on transparent labels.

Many direct marketing experts overwrite the outer envelope of their direct mail package with messages such as ... *great news for dog owners*... or ...*how you can substantially increase the value of your home in under two weeks*.... But while some direct marketers feel it's essential to overprint the outer envelope, others aren't so sure. If you do choose to put a message on your envelopes, make sure it compels the reader to open the envelope and read further. Don't be too catchy or obscure or the direct mail package you worked so hard on might not even get opened.

The order form

Ensure you include everything the reader could possibly need to know on the order form. The less your customer has to do, the more likely they are to order – and sooner. Don't forget to offer options whenever possible, so that people can order by post, phone or fax, and pay by credit card if they want to. All these options need to be clearly shown on the ordering device. Use different paper for the order form, and consider making it a different colour or size from the letter. You'll find more tips on preparing order forms in the next chapter.

Self-addressed envelope

Anything that makes life (and response) easier for the recipient is good news. By enclosing an envelope addressed to yourself you're making it easier and quicker for them to reply. They won't have to hunt around for an envelope or copy out your details. A self-addressed envelope can be as simple as putting your address label on an envelope, or you can overprint them. Make sure the envelope you include is the correct size to enclose what you want returned.

Enclosing a *stamped* self-addressed envelope can increase your chance of a reply from individual consumers who you're writing to at home. Many have found that while it increases response, it doesn't always increase actual sales.

Businesses have franking machines or other methods of paying for outgoing mail, so pre-stamping their return envelopes seems unnecessary.

Timing

The timing of your mailshot is essential, but because each business is different only you can determine which is best for you. There are many pointers you can use to help you decide.

If you're sending mail to home addresses, it's a good idea to have it arrive there on a Saturday (or Friday). This is because during the week, they may work and will end up discarding it rather than have it lying around as yet one more thing to deal with. Weekends, although often full, give many people time to read more.

If you're sending direct mail to a business, try not to have it arrive there on a Saturday or Monday. Mondays are often fraught starts to the working week, with more mail than usual because of the Saturday delivery. So, have it arrive on a Tuesday or later – but not Friday, because by then, people's thoughts are usually of the weekend ahead, and they're trying to clear paperwork from their desks.

Seasonal
Many businesses are seasonal, making them dependent on a lot of trade at a particular time of year. If your business comes into this category, you'll know when your peak sales period is and be able to work dates backwards to see when a mailshot would be the most effective. It also makes a difference whether your prospective customer is an individual or another business. If you make handmade Easter eggs, for example, you may target individuals in early March (depending when Easter falls), but contact businesses much earlier as they need to source and establish availability of products earlier.

July and August are often poor times to target businesses too, as many of their staff are on holiday or covering for absent colleagues. This disruption to normal working does mean that mailshots which would normally be acted upon favourably at other times of the year will often draw a much poorer response.

ANALYSING RESULTS

Depending on what you wanted to achieve from your mailshot, there will be varying lengths of time before you can analyse how well the mailshot worked. If you gave your offer a time limit you will see results much quicker. You must put a source code on your material, however, or you will only be able to guess how many of your sales resulted from the mailshot. When people ring you need to check where they heard about you if you are to gauge your response accurately. Do this (after taking their details) by asking them where they saw the offer, or by reading the response code to you.

Was it cost-effective?
If your mailshot paid for itself, you can say it was cost-effective because not only will you have made enough sales to cover your costs, you will also have raised awareness of your company, product and services. If you keep up the momentum this will lead to more sales in the future. **It is proven that people who are mailed to on a regular basis tend to buy more than those who aren't, so you can see why it's important to keep mailing.**

It is difficult to put a figure on what is a good or excellent response. One commercial illustrator sent out just ten letters. He was contacted by all ten, given work by five and offered a permanent post by another. His secret, he said, was to research carefully who to send the mailshot to, and offer a solution to their problems.

If you send out unsolicited mail to people who aren't already customers, you could be said to be 'cold mailing' and in this instance if you had a 2 per cent response you might say it's good. If you run a large discount furniture store and send out a money-off coupon to 1,000 existing customers in your locality and get back only 50 replies, you may feel it wasn't a worthwhile exercise. Only you can gauge what it cost and what your returns were.

Example
- A discount furniture store sent out 1,000 coupons offering £20 off all sales over £100, valid for one month.
- The cost of printing and posting the voucher and letter was £600.
- 50 people responded and these sales amounted to £10,000.
- The response rate in this example is 5 per cent.
- Their total cost was £1,600 (£600 for the mailshot and £1,000 for 50 x £20 money-off coupons).
- Gross profit equals £8,400.

Other costs to be taken into account are:

- copywriting and design costs of all mailing pieces (if any) and production costs
- list rental.

If you are sending out a large volume of direct mail you may want it to be dealt with by a fulfilment house. Details of these are available from the Direct Marketing Association (see Useful Addresses).

Not cost-effective
If you made a loss on a mailshot you need to analyse why.

Mailed to wrong people
This is usually a good starting point when mailshots go wrong. Are you sure the names and details you had were correct and current? Perhaps you had some returned as people had moved away. Maybe only a small proportion of the people you wrote to were interested in your product or service. Try to salvage something from this exercise by analysing who did respond. Now try to find similar prospects for your next mailing.

When sending to businesses, it's important to get job titles as well as names, then if someone moves post or leaves, you can contact the new post-holder.

Wrong timing
Did you send it out at the right time of year? If so, perhaps it's simply that your potential customer doesn't need what you're offering now. They may have a contract with another supplier which doesn't end until six months time, but if your mailshot and products are good and you continue to keep in touch, they could be renewing their contract with you. Remember, you can't win everyone all the time, but you can always leave a favourable impression.

Unclear messages
Look back over your mailshot. Is it absolutely clear what you were offering? Did you make it clear what action you wanted the reader to take? Read the next chapter to see how to persuade and reassure the undecided reader. Then put yourself in the reader's position – would your offer interest you? If not, why not? Address these issues, but also check your product or service. It's no good providing a service or product people don't want – rephrase it, revise it, or replace it with one they do.

TESTING DIFFERENT ELEMENTS

From the headline you put on the sales letter, to the people you send it to, you can test almost every aspect of a direct mail campaign, including:

- Who you mail it to (age group, sex, marital status, income).

- When you mail it (day of the week, season).

- Various elements of the letter (including salutation, headline, rephrasing offers, guarantees, the PS).

- Offers (free trials, bulk discounts, incentives, buy now and pay later, credit terms, buy one get one free, customer draws, discontinued lines).

- Enclosures (samples, money-off coupons, free offers).

- The ordering process (ordering via phone, fax, credit card facilities, delivery times).

- Selling direct or via a two-step process.

- Envelopes (self-addressed, stamped self-addressed, overprinted).

The important thing to remember is to test only one aspect at a time, otherwise you won't know which change was responsible for the increase (or decrease) in response. One thing is certain, the more direct mail campaigns you do, the better you'll get at instinctively knowing what works and what doesn't. And if something is working consistently well, leave it – don't change anything for change's sake.

MORE TRIED AND TESTED DO'S AND DON'TS

Do

- Make your marketing campaign part of an overall strategy.

- Make regular mailings.

- Test individual elements of a mailing.

- Give people as many different ways to order as possible – by phone, fax, email, post.

- Put a source code on all material so you can be sure where the sale or enquiry originated.

- Ensure you have the necessary infrastructure to respond to your campaign.

- Limit each piece in your mailing to a single objective.

- Make your service or product memorable.

- Go for immediate impact – one or two seconds.

- Limit emphasis, otherwise you accentuate nothing.

- Be aware of all the laws that affect you and keep within them.

Don't

- Try and please everybody.

- Put creativity before clarity.

- Leave things to chance.

- Change things for change's sake.

KEY POINTS

- Small budgets can achieve a lot with direct mail.
- Be specific about who you want to reach.
- Make response easy.
- Retaining existing customers costs less than getting new ones.
- Make information retrieval easier with a computerised database.
- Keep up to date with Data Protection laws.
- Mail people regularly.

5

Write Great Sales Letters

Every letter you write in the course of your business could be considered a sales letter, because every time you write to a customer you are communicating something about you, your product or service, and your company. If you communicate well you'll give them a favourable impression of all three, the result of which may be to keep them as a customer or persuade them to buy from you in the future. There are many uses for sales letters, including:

- selling direct to new or existing customers
- generating enquiries from new or existing customers
- testing new ideas, products and services
- raising funds for a charity or project
- thanking customers for their support or business
- keeping in touch.

In this chapter we'll look at a sales letter as a way of selling by post. Usually it is part of a package, which should include an order or response form and brochure, and may also include testimonials or free samples. In many cases, however, it is simply a letter – a letter that sells!

PLANNING YOUR OUTCOME

A sales letter is a key player in getting business to come to you. One of the major benefits of sales letters is that you choose who gets to hear about your cost-cutting estate agency service, or revolutionary new health care products.

Your sales letter is the postal equivalent of ringing or calling a customer. From their point of view, it's probably the least intrusive way of you contacting them – and if you've chosen your recipients well, they'll welcome the letter. That's because it will inform them of something which will make them healthier or richer or more beautiful or more confident, maybe all of these things, without them having to leave the comfort of their home or office.

It's worth remembering that what people term junk mail is really misdirected mail. If you sent a 70-year-old man details of half-price life insurance which he could take out regardless of age or health he would probably welcome it. Send the same man details of a home pregnancy testing kit and you'd be wasting his time and your money.

Set objectives

When you ring a potential customer with the objective of getting them to buy over the phone, you make sure you have all the details you need to hand, such as price, delivery times and guarantees. It's the same with your letter. So the first thing you ask yourself is what do you want your letter to achieve? Do you want the recipient to ask for more information or to place an immediate order? If it's the latter, make sure you include all ordering information, including an order form, which is looked at in more detail later in this chapter. Before you start to write your letter, however, you have to plan.

Structure your letter

The structure of your sales letter is all important. It's no good starting off with ordering information before you've talked about what's on offer. AIDCA is a tried and tested way of helping you structure your sales letter in the planning stage. It stands for:

Attention
Interest
Desire
Conviction
Action

The idea is that you get your reader's **attention**, which arouses their **interest** in what you're offering, which leads them to **desire** it. You then **convince** them of how good it is before getting them to take **action** (which could be to place an order or phone or write for more information).

Attention

To get your letter read, you must grab your reader's attention immediately. The way to do this is to make your letter relevant to them. It doesn't matter how well written your sales letter is, if it isn't relevant to the reader they'll discard it immediately – and who could blame them? An attention-getting headline at the start of your sales letter is a great way to get straight to the point. In the headline and the first sentence you must say how your product or service will benefit the reader.

Interest
Now you've got them interested, you must maintain momentum and keep them reading. Expand more on the benefit you highlighted in your opening.

Desire
The reader is interested, so now you must create a desire within them to have your product or service. Do this by giving more information, but in such a way they can see exactly how it benefits them. Use emotive words to illustrate how much easier, better, simpler, more beautiful or richer their lives will be if they buy what you're offering.

Conviction
You've got them to read this far. Now convince them that if they order they're doing the right thing. This could be a good time to say how others have benefited from your product or service. Use endorsements and case histories from satisfied customers to help allay any fears your reader has and reinforce guarantees and other things which allow the reader to buy with confidence. You may also like to point out what the reader may lose if they don't buy.

Action
This is it. Be precise about what you expect your reader to do. *Remember to identify the outcome you want before you structure your letter*. If you want them to buy, make it plain, and don't worry about being repetitive. Make sure you give them all the information they need and make everything as clear and as easy as possible.

MAKE IT PERSONAL

One of the great things about writing sales letters is that you can write to people as individuals. You address them personally, by name, which gives you a head start towards building a long and mutually rewarding relationship. It's intimate in a way that TV, radio or press advertising can never be.

So, now you already have a list of people you wish to contact. At the very least you will have their:

Title (Ms, Miss, Mrs, Mr, Dr)
First name
Surname
Job title (if appropriate)
Company name (if appropriate)
Full address.

Ideally, if they are existing customers, you would also have other information to hand, such as their telephone number, how much and when they last ordered. All these things allow you to build up personal profiles of your existing customers. It's amazing how irritated people get about their names and addresses being spelt incorrectly – so make sure you get it right.

When it's not possible to address an individual you can start your letter with:

Dear Friend
Dear Book Lover
Dear Member
Dear Contributor
Dear Patron
Dear Customer
Dear Subscriber

or any other amicable introduction you feel is suitable. Copywriters have different thoughts on which ones work best, but Dear Friend seems to be preferred.

TELL MORE, SELL MORE

You now know who you're going to write to. You have your objectives set and the structure of the letter in mind. You know the benefits your product or service will bring your reader and you're all set to write your sales letter.

It's worth noting here that some of the most successful sales letters are many pages long. Sales letters can't be too long, they can only be too boring. It's no good trying to drag words out to fill more pages than necessary, but if you feel that two or four pages is the natural length of your letter – use them. What you must ensure is that your text flows easily from one word to the next, from one sentence to the next, from one paragraph to the next and so on.

Headlines

The first thing you need to work on is your headline. Because it's so important, you will probably spend at least half – or even as much as 75 per cent – of the time you've allotted to write the whole letter, just on this. We talked about getting attention, and this is your chance. The headline needs to be powerful and appeal to the reader's self-interest. A good headline will greatly increase the response to your offer, so it's worth getting it right. But what makes a good headline? Compare the following two headlines:

DISCOUNT CLOTHING

"Now You Can Look Sensational In Designer Clothes At Chain Store Prices"

The first headline simply states what is on offer. Discount clothing. It could be work overalls, out-of-date stock or poorly made imports. It's dull and doesn't make you want to read further. The second headline, however, conjures up images of designer labels, jeans, jackets, suits, maybe even accessories, all of which you're going to look sensational wearing – and all for the same price you'd pay in a high street chain store. Surely this is worth a read.

When writing headlines in a sales letter, use capital letters at the beginning of all words as you would in advertisements, as this makes it much easier to read:

Upper Case And Lower Case Letters Like This In A Headline

NOT ALL CAPITAL LETTERS LIKE THIS

Curiosity headlines

Curiosity headlines should be used sparingly, if at all. Most people don't have time to play word or mind games when dealing with their mail, so unless your headline compels them to read further they won't bother. Perhaps you've written a report which explains how house purchasers and sellers can do their own conveyancing and save hundreds of pounds. Which headline do you think would draw the biggest response?

WHY DID 3,000 PEOPLE BUY OUR REPORT LAST YEAR?

How To Do Your Own House Conveyancing, Without Expensive Solicitors, For Less Than £180.

The first is an example of a curiosity headline. The second simply and clearly states the benefits to the reader and will almost certainly reap a far bigger response.

'Negative' headlines
Another successful headline strategy can be to pose the reader with a problem – their problem. Perhaps you're offering a special insurance scheme for single parents:

If You Suddenly End Up In Hospital Tomorrow, Who's Going To Take Care Of Your Children?

This would bring a sense of dread to most parents but the secret of using this sort of headline is that you go on to give them the solution. You rescue them and allay their fears.

Misleading headlines
One of the most common ways of using misleading headlines is to introduce sex into the headline. Consider:

AT LAST, SEX AVAILABLE IN THE OFFICE?

The rest of this advertisement may go on to say that now they had the reader's attention, they would get on to the real reason they were writing – training. This form of attracting attention is perceived as trickery and the reader isn't amused, they simply feel cheated. And if they feel you've deceived them from the outset, they won't be inclined to trust anything else you have to say.

Credible headlines
Avoid wild claims when writing headlines – even if they're true. That's because the headline not only has to be true, it has to appear true. If it doesn't you will immediately lose credibility with the reader and they'll think you're overstating and over-selling. Never sell more than you can deliver.

Subheadings

Use lots of subheadings throughout your letter. Visually this breaks up the text and urges the reader forward. You can use one immediately after your headline.

Headline	**For Every Book You Buy From Me**
	I'll Give You Another Absolutely Free
Subheading	*Yes! Free Bonus Book Of Your Choice With Every Book You Order*

Body copy

This is the name given to the rest of the letter. Now that you've got people's attention you can continue to arouse their interest. Do this by expanding on the benefits you've already chosen to highlight and introduce more. Let them know exactly what it is you're offering and most importantly, *what it does for them.*

If you're raising funds for charity, for example, you would hope to move your readers emotionally. You could write case histories, showing how you've helped others to lead better lives. People may be drawn towards helping others if you show that their help really will do something specific – such as their £12 feeding one child for a year. But if you mention that you need £1 billion to support a food aid programme, people will think the little they can give is so insignificant, it's not worth bothering.

Ask for the order

Once you've whetted people's appetite and they want what it is you're offering, you must ask for their order. Call the reader to action.

Testimonials

Now that you've told the reader all that your product can do for them, you need to prove it. How? By using testimonials from satisfied customers. Remember to use the customer's full name and town, such as Mr Richard Reynolds from Swindon, rather than RR from Wiltshire. If you haven't got any testimonials you could always ask some customers who you know are happy with your goods or service to write one for you. Almost always, people are happy to help.

Endorsements

If you're promoting a new product or service and can't supply testimonials, you could ask someone to endorse your product. If you've produced a new car wax polish, for example, you could ask a car valeting company to endorse it

> *... but don't take our word for it, here's what car valeting experts have to say...*

Endorsements or testimonials are more believable than your claims as far as the reader is concerned.

Guarantees

Offer guarantees – *free 30-day trial period* – to reassure the reader and then get your reader to act. Give a reason (or reasons) why the reader should buy now and not in two months' time.

> *...place your order within the next seven days and get fitted valance sheet free* and *order within fifteen days and get frilled pillowcase free...*

You're doing this in an attempt to get people to act immediately. Urge people not to delay by pointing out what they'll miss if they don't order quickly. It's worthwhile remembering, however, that the item you offer free must be something people would buy. You can't give away what you can't sell.

Signing off

When you come to the end of the letter, make sure it is from a specific person – not a department. Practise signing your name in full, if you don't already – John Letchworth, not J D Letchworth for example – and make sure it's legible.

Sign your sales letters in blue fibre tip pen – tests show this is best. If you're printing so many copies you can't possibly sign them personally, ask your printer to print your signature in reflex blue ink.

PS

People often read the PS before they read the letter. After the headline it's the most read part of the letter. All sales letters should have a PS, as it often doubles response. Sometimes, if it's warranted they'll have a PPS too. In the PS you need to restate your offer. If you're selling a greenhouse, for example, you could write:

PS Buy within fourteen days and the staging comes free. Order within seven days and you'll also earn a special bonus of a greenhouse irrigation system.

CHOOSE WORDS CAREFULLY

You need to write words that sell – and every word you write in a sales letter or an advertisement has to earn its living. When preparing your first drafts simply let the words flow onto the page. Don't interrupt the flow by editing at this stage, you can restructure and eliminate superfluous text later.

When writing you always need to have your typical reader in mind. Are they industrialists, upwardly mobile young professionals, or young consumers? Whoever they are, your writing style must suit them and their tastes. If you're writing to computer programmers they may well understand what's meant by RAM, MHz or HTML, but to anyone else this would be considered technospeak, so avoid it at all costs.

Self-indulgence
How many times have you opened a letter only to be bombarded with facts about a person or company. For instance:

Dear Mrs Grant

We're celebrating our success

Established over 50 years ago, Mason and Sons has remained a family business ever since that time. Now, due to our success, we are relocating to larger premises on the outskirts of Manchester. We are proud to say that William Mason, grandson of the founder, will . . .

This is company indulgent writing and of no interest to the reader, certainly not at the opening of your letter.

Remember never to write about how great you are, but do say to your reader, 'This is what we can do for you.'

Specifics
Be specific when describing your product or service. Would you

rather buy a 'holiday home' or 'a cedarwood chalet nestling on a wooded hillside overlooking Lyme Bay'?

If you're talking about a product being faster or lasting longer, again be specific. Faster or longer than...? Its nearest rival? A previous model?

Whatever you write, be truthful. You are obliged to ensure it is so. Besides, if just one of your claims is shown to be exaggerated or false, your whole credibility will be undermined.

Don't write passively. Instead of writing, *Your hopes can be realised in one week,* write, *Be a qualified driver in less than five days!*

Style

You will undoubtedly develop your own style, but there are certain things which every writer of sales material should avoid. Don't use elaborate phrases when one word will suffice. Say *Now*, for example, not *at this point in time.* Say *decide* instead of *come to a decision as to.*

Look at your choice of words. Use colourful emotive words to encourage your reader to respond. Short words and sentences make for ease of reading, but don't make everything too short or stilted for the sake of it, or your work won't flow or have rhythm. Don't introduce words that stop your reader mid-read. An example of this is:

> *we offer a guarantee (see attached certificate)*

as the reader may turn to the certificate and stop reading the letter and lose the flow.

Editing

When you have finished your letter and feel reasonably happy with it, you can start editing. Put it to one side for a day, if possible, before reading it through to yourself and answering the following questions:

- Is it suitable for the audience you have in mind?
- Does it flow?
- Is it believable?
- Is it truthful?
- Is it clear?
- Is it emotive?
- Would it make you act?

If the answer to any of these questions is no, revise the letter.

HOW SHOULD IT LOOK?

The layout of your letter is important. Many well-written sales letters have failed to raise the desired response because of the way they looked to the reader. Much research has been carried out on how to make letters more readable. By adopting the following guidelines you can greatly improve the chances of your sales letters being read and acted upon.

Headed paper

Don't send sales letters on your usual headed paper as nothing should come before the compelling headline you've spent so long perfecting. When writing dedicated sales letters, put your company information, name, address, telephone and fax numbers, logo, email and website addresses, if you have them, at the bottom of the last page. Use a reasonable quality paper (80 gsm, perhaps) or a higher grade.

Which typestyle?

You need to use a typestyle (font) that's easy to read. Using a typeface which has a serif is better than one without. The following examples show the difference:

Serif fonts, such as this, are easier to read.

Sans serif fonts, such as this, are more difficult to read.

You'll notice the top (serif) typeface has small strokes on its letters which improve readability, especially when there is a lot of text together as in a letter. You can use sans serif fonts in a headline if you wish as these are usually printed larger and contain far fewer words. But to read a whole letter or document written in a sans serif font is difficult on the eye.

Many successful marketers recommend using a typeface known as Courier for the body of all their sales letters. However, they still use a serif font such as Times Roman or Times New Roman for their headlines.

This is the typeface known as Courier.

Do not have long blocks of text throughout your letter. Break them up into small paragraphs and have plenty of subheadings. The subheading can simply be in bolder type and slightly larger. Don't be tempted to use fancy fonts or lots of different fonts – it looks garish and amateurish.

Laying out text on the pages

The overall look of your letter is crucial. Using short paragraphs and plenty of subheadings is excellent to break up text, but there are many other tips to help keep your reader interested.

> Look at this paragraph. It is justified which means that the end of every line finishes at the same point. This makes long tracts of text more difficult to read. When modern typewriters and computers gave people the ability to justify text, everyone started using it, but it really does make documents, letters, brochures and books more difficult to read, so most people have returned to the following:
>
> This paragraph is printed with a ragged right edge. This means that all the lines start flush with the left but don't all end at the same place on the right. In addition, you don't get large white gaps between words as you do in the justified example above.

You can also alter the width of your paragraphs to add interest to your letter. The above two paragraphs are a different width from the ones preceding and following them, which adds interest to the page. By breaking the text up in this way, your reader won't think they have so much to trawl through, so they'll be encouraged to read on and not discard your letter.

When coming to the bottom of each page of your letter, don't finish at the end of a sentence. Break it to arouse interest and continue it on the following page to ensure readers go to page two, and so on. Here is an example of how you could so this:

```
money-saving device which will make you the envy of
all your neighbours. But that's not all . . .
```

Then you could continue the sentence on the next page as follows:

```
if you order within seven days, I'll send you a
recharger (worth £17) absolutely free.
```

Margin notes

You may have received letters which have handwritten notes in the margin. Usually these are written by the same person who signs the letter. Just as they sign the letter in blue, so these notes should be written in blue. You can draw arrows to them from an old price you've crossed out in the text, for example, but remember to use this device sparingly.

Managing eye-track

There are certain points in your letter to which people's eyes will be automatically drawn. Studies of eye-track management have shown that when people are looking at an A4 piece of paper their eyes come in at the top left and leave bottom right, whereas on an A3 piece of paper the eyes come in top right and leave bottom right. This is why many advertising agencies insist their clients' adverts are placed on the right-hand page of a magazine, preferably at the top right.

Your reader will glance at the sales letter extremely rapidly, so along the path from where their eyes come in to where they go out, you need to create fixing points. Examples could include:

- headline
- photographs
- illustrations or diagram
- subheadings
- bullet points
- highlighted text
- handwritten notes
- boxed or bordered text.

You can see therefore why it is essential to create compelling headlines and subheadings and why it is vital to pay attention to the layout of your letter. If you haven't, it doesn't matter how well you've written the letter, within seconds of it being opened, it could be hurtling towards the wastepaper basket.

MAKE ORDERING EASY

If you want your reader to order after reading your offer, you must include an order form. Making everything easy for your reader is especially true when designing the order form. Sometimes people pick up the order form or card before even reading the letter, so make sure it summarises the letter.

The order form

You need to plan and write the order form as carefully as you do your sales letter. Many marketers do this before the letter as it helps them condense and encapsulate the best of what they're offering. Make it look good, and as exciting as possible. Let people feel confident they're making the right choice.

Ensure you have everything they'll possibly need to know on the order form, and make sure it's consistent with the information in your letter. Don't say *Send No Money Now* if you've said *Money Back If Not Absolutely Delighted* in your letter.

It should have a title, what you're offering and guarantees. In addition you could bullet-point major benefits of your product or service. It may be paper or card, and you can choose the size, but make it look different from the letter, by using a different colour paper for instance.

The less your customer has to do, the more likely they are to order – and sooner. Use tick boxes to make their life easier and, if practical, print their name and address on the order form before mailing out. If customers can pay by credit card, so much the better – allow space for these details too, and make it clear whether postage and packing is included. Repeat *your* name, address and telephone number on the order form and offer options whenever possible, so that people can order by phone, fax or post. Make sure these options are shown on the ordering device. Make it look good, something special – it is a very important document.

KEY POINTS

Before writing your sales letter:

- Define your objective.
- Plan carefully.
- Make it personal.
- Write clearly and concisely.
- Ensure the letter flows.
- Write honest and believable copy.
- Consider the layout and typeface.
- Make ordering easy and risk-free.

6

How To Sell To Customers Again and Again

Make people a priority, and they change from being prospective customers to actual customers. And if you put customer relations before a quick profit you can go on selling to the same customer over and over again. When you combine excellent marketing and customer service with an outstanding product or service your business will really take off. On average, customers spend three times more in their fourth year than in their first, and it costs less to keep an existing customer than to find a new one.

GROWING CUSTOMER RELATIONSHIPS

Why do your customers choose to spend their money with you as opposed to someone else? Is it because you have an excellent product, or because you deliver when others don't, or offer credit facilities when others demand full and immediate payment? Or is it because your competitors simply don't market themselves as well as you do so your customers aren't even aware they exist? There's no denying that all these things play a part. When a customer buys from you for the first time, however, they may not be considering buying from you in the future. Perhaps you just happened to fill a need there and then – motorway service stations are an example of this. If you live in Bristol you won't drive all the way to Blackpool every time you need to refuel, no matter how good the service is – but you may well tell others who are travelling that way.

The importance of growing excellent customer relations cannot be emphasised enough. If you go to a restaurant and the food is wonderful but the staff are unfriendly and unhelpful, would you go back? If you visit a restaurant where the food is mediocre, but the staff go out of their way to ensure you have an enjoyable meal and visit, you may overlook the less than perfect food. Imagine, then, a restaurant where the food is great, the staff are courteous and helpful and treat you as if you're their most valued customer – wouldn't you go back again and again?

Going the extra mile

On a dark winter's evening, a local garage was about to close when an elderly gentleman drove his car in with a flat tyre. He was in a terrible state as he was due to pick his wife up from outside the coach station over three miles away in less than ten minutes. The owners of the garage didn't hesitate. One gave the man a lift to the bus station to collect his wife and by the time they returned the other had fixed the puncture. The only charge they made was for the cost of fixing the puncture. For many, this may seem like a poor business decision, and based on the value of that single transaction it was. But, the elderly couple were so delighted at the garage owners' kindness that they contacted the local newspaper. A local reporter interviewed the garage owners who said, 'We only did what we hope someone would do for our parents if they ever got stuck like that.' Thereafter their sales rocketed – not only did the elderly couple take their car there for servicing, but so did their children, grandchildren and friends, as well as many other local people who'd read about the garage owners who'd gone the extra mile.

Going the extra mile is a mindset!

If you're looking to squeeze every last penny out of every transaction, and give the least you can get away with in return, it's unlikely you'll win awards for customer service. Many business owners believe they lose customers to competitors because their competitors offer the same thing but cheaper. You may be surprised to hear that one of the main reasons people move their business from one supplier to another is because of the indifference shown to them by their current supplier.

So, pay attention to detail, treat every customer like a brand new customer and *always* do a great job. Return their phone calls within hours and their letters within days – even if it's only an acknowledgement. Deliver on time, meet deadlines and never promise anything you can't deliver. Put problems right, exchange faulty goods, compensate for poor workmanship, redo a less than perfect job, add something extra and ask for suggestions on how you can make things even better. Give your most loyal customers preferential treatment and if they're in business, go out of your way to help them by recommending clients too. Give *excellent* customer service as standard.

Promise less, deliver more
If you sell someone a greenhouse, try to deliver more than a greenhouse. Why not send a few seed trays with it, complete with packets of seeds? Your customers will be delighted you've added something as a goodwill gesture. Tell them you've included the free gift because they're a loyal customer, or your first customer, or because it's their first order. Whichever way you choose to do it – deliver more than you sell.

Encourage customer loyalty
Show your customers how much you appreciate their loyalty. Say that you're giving them 20 per cent off their latest invoice because they're such valued customers. Offer them discounts against future purchases too – perhaps a £10 voucher redeemable against their next purchase – anything which lets them know exactly how much you value them as customers.

Long-term investment
If you think that you can't afford to give away extra goodies and money off, try viewing these 'giveaways' in a different way. If you consider the lifetime value of a customer, one you can sell to again and again, the cost of your giveaways will be recouped many times. Besides, you may be able to get suppliers of associated goods to give you samples or products at a much greater discount. After all, your success could be their success, and it's a way of drawing attention to their products and services.

In the case of money-off vouchers, the customer can only redeem these if they spend with you again. And that's what you're trying to achieve, getting the same customers to purchase your services time and time again. That's because it's much easier, and more cost-effective, to market your services to an existing customer than spend larger sums of money trying to attract new ones.

Don't frustrate buyers
If you sell a special craft ink, but not the special type of paper you need to use it on, tell the customer. Don't let them get all the way home only to discover they can't use the ink because they don't have

the special paper. It's you they'll be irritated with for not pointing it out – not the ink manufacturer. Perhaps it's worth stocking and selling the paper yourself. If not, find out who does and point your customer in their direction, or stock small samples that you've obtained from the supplier. The customer will be grateful for your consideration and help, as will the supplier.

Offer options

Imagine you sell DIY products, and someone comes in for a paintbrush. Make conversation, ask them what they're painting and give them options. The first option could be just to buy the brush. The second could be the brush and paint. The third could be paint, brush, roller and tray. Don't make a single offer, give people the options and choice and invariably they'll go for the one in the middle. So, when a customer comes to you, ask what they need your product for and offer them a tiered set of solutions.

Whatever you're selling, try to think of ways in which you can give your customers added value. This may be in the form of free delivery, or extended warranty, or you can offer bundled goods, free subscriptions, or a money-off voucher for future use.

OFFER GUARANTEES

To get the best response from your sales messages you need to minimise risk on behalf of your customer. The best way to do this is to offer them guarantees. Perhaps an elderly couple won't respond to a double-glazing advert because they're worried pushy sales-people will call at their home. So you write:

No salespeople will call – guaranteed!

People are always concerned they may end up paying for something they really don't want. You can allay their fears by writing statements such as:

I'll post you this neck pillow to examine FREE in the comfort of your own home.
Send no money now.
Test our neck pillow for 7 days – then decide!
You never risk a penny.

Or, if they pay with order, things such as:

If you're not absolutely delighted, I'll immediately buy it back – no questions asked.

Everyone likes guarantees. You like to know that if your new computer is faulty it will be exchanged without question; if your washing machine breaks down, it will be fixed promptly; and if the wellington boots you bought through mail order don't fit, you can return them for a full unequivocal refund.

Guarantee your customers that if a product or service doesn't live up to their expectations they won't be out of pocket. Offering guarantees can increase response.

Offering a money back guarantee always increases response.

So, if you're writing a sales letter, for instance, include phrases such as:

I personally guarantee that if you're not absolutely delighted your money will be promptly refunded – no questions asked.

Or:

I guarantee this organiser will bring order to your busy schedule. If, after examining its contents, however, you're not 100% satisfied, please return it to me within 90 days for a full, no questions asked, refund.

You may think that 90 days is too long a period for your customer to return your product – but this isn't so. The longer the guarantee period, the longer your customer has to test your products and services, and to discover how wonderful they are. It may also be that because they have such a long period, they forget to return them. Either way, the longer the guarantee period you offer, the less returns you'll have. And by saying things such as *a full no-questions-asked refund* or *a no-quibble refund* you let the customer know they're not going to have to come up with reasons why they don't want your product after trying it, which again makes them far more likely to order.

You don't have to offer just one guarantee. You can offer multiple guarantees, such as:

> *With Scott's Contract Security Services I personally guarantee:*
>
> *1. No rise in contract rates for next two years.*
> *2. 24-hour emergency service – 365 days a year.*
> *3. If we take longer than 15 minutes to respond to your call – I'll pay your next month's premium for you.*
>
> *That's my promise. And remember, you can cancel your contract with me at any time.*

The above is a great example of how good multiple guarantees can be for your marketing efforts. If you wanted to engage contract security services, wouldn't you be keen to test Scott's Security? After all, what do you have to lose? And that's what you need to do – constantly reassure your customers and potential customers by offering guarantees. Legally you're obliged to deliver what you offer anyway, so make a virtue of the fact.

Remember never to offer something you can't deliver.

OWN UP TO MISTAKES

By putting reliable people and systems in place you will obviously greatly reduce the risk of mistakes being made in your business, but however well you run your business, things can occasionally go wrong. Mix-ups over orders, payments, refunds, deliveries, briefs, schedules, deadlines, instructions, repairs, servicing contracts and information are just some of the things that can catch you out. Far from being disastrous, this can be a wonderful opportunity for you to prove to your customer just how much their business really means to you, in a way they probably never even realised before. That's assuming you get to hear of the complaint, **because a staggering 94 per cent of customers don't even bother to complain – they simply walk away**. They'll stop buying your products or services with no explanation at all. Add to this the fact that the average customer with a complaint will also tell nine other people and you can see why it really is worth making the effort to get things right.

Feedback
Because of these startling facts, you need to positively encourage regular feedback from your customers. Depending on the number of

customers you have, and the resources and time you have available, you can do this in many ways, including:

- *Personal contact* – a great way to build a good open relationship with a customer. Be sure to make it easy for your customer to offer negative feedback too. Explain how it will help you offer an even better service than you do already.

- *Telephone contact* – phone a customer and say that you're ringing to see if they're happy with your product or service and to ask if there's any way in which you could make it even better for them. Could you make it easier for them to order, for instance? Explain it's a courtesy call as you really do value their custom.

- *Letter* – again, the same principles apply. Make response easy – attach a questionnaire (not too lengthy) complete with tick boxes so they can quickly and easily rate different aspects of your service. Offer them an incentive to respond early, perhaps entry into a draw or money off their next order. Include a prepaid self-addressed envelope or offer a fax-back facility.

- *Response card with every order* – this could be a preprinted card which carries as many standard details as possible with spaces and tick boxes for your customers to rate your services. Again, you could offer an incentive.

- *Newsletter* – an extremely useful way to keep in touch with your potential and existing customer base. Ask them to contribute suggestions as to how you can improve services or products, or offer tips on how to get the best from both. The frequency and format of the newsletter will again depend on resources.

Some of these methods will work better than others depending on a variety of factors which are unique to you and your business. But don't push this too far down your list of priorities, because:

> **If you don't take care of your customers, someone else will.**

One of the challenges you face is in realising that a customer has left you.

Remember that 94 per cent of customers won't complain, they'll simply take their business elsewhere without telling you. If you don't notice this, you'll be guilty of one of the reasons customers switch suppliers – indifference. Many business owners believe their customers defect because they can get the same goods or services cheaper elsewhere, but this only accounts for a minority of defections. **Indifference on the part of their existing supplier is the main reason customers switch.**

Deal successfully with complaints

Because of the wide variety of complaints people can make, the following is a general rule of the stages you need to move through to deal with a complaint successfully:

- *Acknowledge the complaint* – preferably personally, on the telephone or by return of post.

- *Assure the customer* you are doing everything possible to reach a satisfactory conclusion.

- *Tell the customer* that you will get back to them by a specific date, and even if you haven't managed to resolve the issue by then, contact them to reassure them you're doing everything possible.

- *Give your name* as the person to contact – don't hide behind a faceless organisation.

- *Gather information* – retrace the complaint and gather all necessary information from people and paperwork.

- *Make a decision* – once certain you're in possession of all the facts, make a decision as to how you're going to handle the complaint. Remember to:
  - make this a damage limitation exercise
  - come out of it looking good whether the complaint was justified or not
  - give the customer the benefit of the doubt where there is any
  - put yourself in your customer's shoes and see the situation from their angle
  - act courteously, kindly and generously at all times, even if you find the customer's complaint was unjustified.

- *Act promptly* – ring or write to the customer as soon as possible informing them how you're going to rectify the situation.

- *Add something extra* – a bunch of flowers, a personal card, a box of chocolates, a money-off voucher, a freebie – whatever it takes to show the customer just how much you value them.

- *Hold a solutions-oriented meeting* – get together with your team (or yourself if it's just you) to look at ways you can avoid that particular situation arising again. Now put the answers into practice.

When is a mistake not a mistake?

What can be a mistake in your customer's eyes, however, may not be as far as you're concerned. You may believe you did what your customer requested, as did a hair salon in Newton Abbot.

One of their loyal customers, Lynn, regularly had cuts, trims and restyles, but on one visit asked for streaks to be put in her hair. As it was the first time she'd asked for this, the stylist went through the options of colour and intensity. Erring on the side of caution, Lynn decided on a few streaks one or two shades lighter than her natural colour, and once finished she paid happily and went home.

Looking at herself in the mirror at home, Lynn decided that her hair really didn't look that much different, so she rang the salon and asked to speak to the manager. She explained that she'd paid out for something which really didn't look significantly different.

'Believe me, I'm not usually one to complain,' she added.

'No, you're not complaining,' the salon manager said courteously. 'There's simply been an error in communication. Now, how soon can you come back to have it redone completely free of charge?'

The next day Lynn returned to the salon, had considerably more streaks put in her hair and was, as usual, treated with great courtesy, and offered coffee and mints. She left a happy lady and not only returned regularly, as usual, but told many of her friends about how well the salon had handled her 'complaint'. As a result of this the salon gained several new customers. It could have been a completely different story if the salon had said that she got exactly what she asked for and refused to do anything further.

GETTING CUSTOMERS TO WORK WITH YOU

Great service yields satisfied customers, and satisfied customers tell colleagues, neighbours, family, contacts and friends just how great/reasonable/conscientious/quick/safe/time-saving/money-saving you or your products and services are. So, in providing exceptional service and products and outstanding customer relations you already have people promoting your business. However, there are other, more structured ways in which you can get your customers actively seeking new business on your behalf. By turning your customers into valuable members of your sales team, you can start reaping the additional benefits of this approach.

Benefit others

So how can you get them working with you? Imagine you run an accountancy and bookkeeping service and are called in to sort out the appalling accounts and accounting system of a small plumbing business. The plumbing company's proprietor has been a one-person business for many years, muddling through with accounts as best he could. Business has been so good, however, he decided to expand, and has recently taken on three staff – a secretary and two service engineers. The plumber's accounting system can no longer cope, nor can the plumber. Following his plea, you set up a computerised accounting system and train him and his secretary to use it with ease. Then you get his past records up to date and set up systems to ensure they can all keep things that way. The plumber is thrilled.

Make sure the customer is happy

Once you're confident the plumber is happy with what you've done, take some time to go over the benefits of your work with him: his peace of mind at getting tax returns prepared on time, which means he saves on interest; his increased cash flow as a result of keeping on top of invoices and bad payers. He's got more time now too, as his secretary can deal with all the accounts. At the touch of a key he can check his bank balances, saving him unnecessary fees from going beyond his agreed overdrafts. Yes, he's very happy, and feeling good about you and your company.

Now you can ask: 'I imagine you know other small businesses who would benefit from my service in the way you've done.'

It's virtually guaranteed that your customer will know several people in the same position as himself. Ask if he can give you names, which invariably he'll be happy to do. Then ask: 'It's alright for me to use your name when I call them, isn't it?' Again, in the vast majority of cases, he'll agree readily.

Now when you call the people he's referred you to, you can mention his name, which is a much better way to gain more business than to cold call. They know that the plumber is delighted with what you've done and that you can benefit them in the same way.

You can do this with every one of your clients and customers. If each referred just three other businesses, think how this would boost your income and customer base – with hardly any additional outlay.

Always remember to call or write to the original referee and thank them for their help, even if the people they referred didn't need your services. It keeps you in contact and shows your gratitude – and you can ask for referrals again and again.

KEY POINTS

- Make people a priority.
- Treat *every* customer like a new customer.
- Promise less, deliver more.
- Build open relationships, encourage feedback.
- Complaints result from poor communication.
- Customer service is a mindset.

7

Use Proven Telephone Techniques

THE POWER OF THE PHONE

The power of the telephone is amazing, and the way you use it speaks volumes about you and your business. How long it takes you to answer, what you say, and how you say it, tells the caller a great deal – and it's the same with outgoing calls.

Your set up is unique. You may answer all calls yourself, have staff who answer, use an answering machine or service, or use an outside agency. If other people in your business use the phone, they also need to be aware of how important it is to develop telephone skills.

Every time the telephone rings, it's an opportunity to do business.

Consider some of the reasons you might use the telephone:

- to answer enquiries
- to deal with invoice queries
- to make appointments
- as an after-sales courtesy call
- to deal with a complaint
- to retrieve lost customers
- to sell
- to take orders
- to chase up overdue accounts.

These are just some of the reasons you may use the telephone, and every one of them gives you an opportunity to do more business, either in the short, mid or long term.

The things that you say

The following are examples of just some of the things people say on the telephone:

● *'No, Mr Graham left ages ago. Sorry. Bye.'* [hangs up]

Because the caller asked for someone who once worked in the company, it's very likely that they wanted to speak to Mr Graham in his position as sales manager. Result – lost business.

● *'She'll be out of the office for the rest of the week. Try calling back Monday, she should be here by then.'*

The caller should have been asked the nature of her enquiry in case there was someone else who could help her. If not, her contact details should have been taken with the assurance she would be called back. Result – possible lost business.

● Phone answered with: *'Yes...'*

This sounds unprofessional and off-putting and will result in wasted time on the caller's behalf trying to establish whether they've called the correct number. Result – possible lost business.

● *'The order line is engaged – give it a try later. I'm on my own, y'see and it's always hectic on Thursdays. Better still, try again tomorrow.'*

Again, no attempt was made to see who was calling or to take their contact details with an offer to return the call. The caller doesn't need to know the company's staffing limitations either. The caller will probably ring a competitor who can take their order straight away. Result – lost business.

● *'No, it's not worth our while to supply anything in such small quantities...'*

This sounds dismissive and patronising. Imagine the difference if the person answering the call said: *'I'm happy to give you the number of a company who can deliver those quantities direct to your door.'* Result – favourable impression given of the company because they're willing to help people, even to the extent that they've bothered to find out the number of a similar company who can help smaller businesses. When those small businesses grow, they'll remember the first class service they got from their first contact and tell others too.

● *'Sorry for the wait, but we're experiencing staffing problems...'*

The caller isn't interested in the problems of the company they are trying to ring, they're interested only in finding a solution to their own problems. Take their contact details and offer to return the call if the wait continues.

The above are only a few examples of how people unknowingly project a poor image of themselves and their organisation.

And the *way* that you say it

But it's not just what you say, it's also the way you say it that matters. The tone of your voice, your posture and your mood all have an impact on the way you sound on the telephone, regardless of what you say. If you have a set way of answering the telephone, such as:

> *Good afternoon, XYZ Limited, Michael speaking, how can I help you?*

This will sound different according to the way you speak. If you said this in an insincere tone which suggested you were reeling it out for the 1,000th time that day, the caller would pick up on it and associate that same attitude with your organisation.

Make the most of your voice. Be pleasant, authoritative and smile. Even though they can't see you, a smile sounds in the voice.

Interruption or opportunity?

When the telephone rings, do you see it as an interruption; as something else that will take you away from what you're doing? If so, that's how others in your company will view it – as a nuisance, an interruption – and that's how the caller will perceive it too. You need to set a great example whenever you use the phone, and always answer calls which are for you.

Some days you may feel that the day has passed without you being able to complete anything because the phone kept ringing all day. However, if customers and potential customers want to speak with you, it makes sense to make them a priority. They're the reason you're in business. If you feel you would be more productive doing other things, consider having someone answer the phone on your behalf. If you're doing something which needs intense concentration and you really don't want interruptions, you might find it better to leave instructions for others to answer the phone on your behalf, or work away from your usual place of work.

One-stop solution
Avoid passing customers from one person to another as this can prove extremely frustrating for the caller. By keeping good links between the different sections of your business, any one person can try to deal with all the caller's queries to avoid passing them from person to person. If this isn't possible, tell the caller you will get your colleague to ring them back, and be responsible for ensuring this happens. Give the caller your name too, so that if the caller does ring back, they don't have to go through the frustrating process of speaking to yet another person and having to explain the issues again.

TELEPHONE OPPORTUNITIES

In the last two years people have started to use the phone more for shopping, making enquiries and paying their bills. Eighty per cent of consumers now say they feel confident about doing their banking, sorting out their insurance and buying goods by phone. The type of business you're in will determine your phone use. If you invite telephone sales for goods which you later mail, for example, you would use the phone more than if you owned a walk-in leather repair shop.

> **When people ring you they make a decision in seconds about you and your company.**

The way you use the telephone will help you make or lose sales, and give people a favourable or unfavourable opinion of you. If you are responsible for answering your own telephone, you need to give people the right impression when you answer. If someone else is responsible (and several different people might be), it's essential they are all aware of the importance of the telephone and become familiar with basic telephone techniques.

The telephone presents wonderful opportunities for every small business, and uses can include the following:

List cleaning
Whatever size your business, you will keep records, including details of people you sell to. People and businesses move, so keep up to date with their current addresses. Within organisations, people leave or are promoted, demoted, made redundant or retire, so you need to

have the details of the person and department who has replaced your old contact. Occasionally what was once a buying decision for a product development manager might be transferred to a marketing manager, so it's important you address new material to them instead.

If you are calling just to check whether Sue Tarleton is still the finance director, clarify small details such as this with the telephone operator. Always check the spelling to ensure you get names and addresses correct as a wrong spelling implies carelessness on your part. And if they say the new director is Sam Billman or Chris Sargent, check whether they're male or female.

Research

This is a great way to find out more about potential and existing customers and a very useful way to gather information. If you're offering a graphic design service, for instance, and need to find out who in a company would make the decision to use you, call the company and explain what it is you need. You may find yourself put through to different people before you find the right one, but nonetheless, it will be worthwhile in the end. Now when you send that sales letter or brochure, you can be sure you're sending it to the right person, and you will probably have picked up one or two other useful pointers during your call too.

This can be preferable to writing, as a written response by its very nature takes more time, and people are often reluctant to commit to paper comments which they will say readily over the phone.

People often say things over the phone they wouldn't put in writing.

If you do want a name and the switchboard operator says they can't tell you because of company policy, reassure them that you only want to write to the person, not call them. Explain you are in business and need to ensure that your letter gets to the right person. If this doesn't work, try ringing at a different time, asking for another department. The person there may not be so aware of 'company policy' and be happy to help you, and ultimately their company too.

Following up leads

Imagine you've written to, or called, a company for information about their products and services. They send you the relevant material quickly and follow it up a short while later with an interesting non-pushy phone call. That company is demonstrating how interested they are in your business, and may well be able to answer questions about their products which have been troubling you. When you decide to buy you will be influenced by how you have been dealt with from your initial enquiry to date. It makes sense therefore to respond with equal care to sales enquiries and actual sales.

Telephone calls can double the amount of appointments generated from a direct mail campaign.

The benefits of following up your direct mail with a telephone call are numerous. Not only does it allow you to reinforce the messages you mailed, it allows you to confirm details, handle queries, and altogether show how efficient and customer-oriented you are. If you are getting a lot of queries during these calls, look again at what you're sending out, as it may be that your copy needs to be reworded and made plainer.

And if you've sent a direct mail package to an existing customer, for instance, which shows you're reducing your turn-round time from seven days to three days, guaranteed, try saying something such as: '*How do you think our guaranteed three-day turn round will improve your business . . . ?*' instead of asking him if he's had a chance to read the package you sent.

Care calls (sometimes referred to as account management)

The number of customers you have will determine how often you can call them. But it's wise to make this contact a priority. Many small businesses, and one-person service providers, adopt a 'let sleeping dogs lie' attitude to customers, believing that if they call to see if everything is OK they may well be told it isn't. If this is the case, it is much better you listen to their grievances and do something about it. More often than not, the customer will be pleasantly surprised to hear from you and feel good that you value them enough to take the time and trouble to call.

> **Speak to your existing customers and you'll increase their loyalty.**

Above all, listen to your customers, look out for trends and use this to continually improve your products and services.

Making appointments

When you use the telephone to make appointments for yourself or a member of your team to visit a prospective client, you need to handle the call well. If you are pushy or forceful, the person you are calling will believe your sales team and sales methods are too, and refuse the appointment. If you are trying to make an appointment for someone to discuss a product or service for which they clearly have no desire or need, you are wasting their time, your own time, and even more of your salesperson's time and resources.

> **Do not make the mistake of trying to sell.**
> **Create interest, arrange an appointment.**

Let the person you are calling know how long your salesperson will need to spend with them and take details of where they are. Most companies now have a map of their location which they can fax to you. Thank the person for agreeing to the salesperson calling and say you will telephone again after the visit to check progress.

Response calls

If you've put your telephone number on your advertisements for people to ring for orders and enquiries, you must ensure you can handle the response well. Otherwise you will have wasted a great deal of money generating enquiries you can't deal with.

One small company which makes painted children's furniture placed small display advertisements in the classified sections of various homestyle magazines.

When people call in response to their advert and ask, *'What colour and designs do you have the children's toy chest in?'* they answer, *'What colour and design would you like it in?'*

The owner of the company says: 'This way we're not losing custom because we only produce bird designs in blue when people want bear designs in yellow.' So, welcome all questions and understand them before you answer.

If you hope to convert these incoming enquiries into immediate sales, you need to be well prepared, have answers at your fingertips and, in most instances, be able to take payment over the phone.

SALES CALLS

Telemarketing (which simply means using the telephone for marketing purposes) can provide great opportunities for the small business. You can telephone people you already do business with or people you'd like to do business with. In the same way that you send sales letters to people who you consider would be interested in your products or services, so you choose to ring people who are. It is particularly effective when you target the right people. You can choose to use telemarketing for a number of reasons, including selling direct over the phone or to make appointments for representatives to call. Or it might be as a follow-up call to a recent mailshot that you sent out. Using the telephone in this way can greatly increase the effectiveness of your mailshot as your information is still fresh in people's minds – and they have at least heard of you. Often people mean to respond to advertisements or sales letters, but simply don't get around to it and for this reason they're pleased you've called.

Getting over the fear

For many people the prospect of making a sales call is terrifying. However, as thousands have discovered, the more calls you make, the better you become at it, and you do get to enjoy it. Besides, you're not really selling, you're providing a valuable service by linking people with what they want and giving them an opportunity to make money, feel healthier, save time or whatever it is you're offering. Make your call interesting, relevant, friendly and they'll want to talk. If you're feeling really nervous about making a call, try:

- breathing deeply through your nose
- shrugging and dropping your shoulders a few times
- closing your eyes and visualising the outcome you want
- smiling.

Now, go ahead and make that call.

While you don't want your conversations to sound too contrived, it does pay to make a note of key points before making a call. This helps you build up confidence and gives your call structure. You need to sound confident – if you sound unsure about what you're offering and its value, you'll transmit this to the person on the other end, regardless of what you actually say. If you're asked something which you don't know the answer to, say you'll find out and call back. You won't make a sale with every call, but if you handle the call well, you will leave a favourable impression of you, your company and the way it values customers and does business.

Structure your call

As a guide, during the first half of the phone call you should do 75 per cent of the listening, and in the second half 75 per cent of the talking.

- Before you ring – have a clear objective *and* have the customer's records handy.

- As you ring – smile.

- Introduce yourself immediately and say why you're calling.

- Gather information.

- Develop a two-way understanding.

- Listen, and check your understanding.

- Discuss how you can help.

- Offer something relevant and interesting to them.

- Leave them with a favourable impression.

Always smile, be positive, be enthusiastic and be yourself.

Questioning techniques

Skilled questioning will elicit information in a conversational way.

- Use open-ended questions to encourage them to talk about themselves, their business and their needs. These questions usually begin with: *who, what, when, where, which, how* and *why* (use *why* sparingly).

- Use a variety of openings:
  - flattery (*you obviously have a lot of experience in...*)
  - information (*could you tell me...*)

- opinion (*what are your thoughts about . . .*)
- idea *(I've been thinking . . .)*
- curiosity (*I've often wondered . . .*)
- testimonials *(ABC Mail Order halved their returns using our . . .)*
- interest (*I was interested to see that your . . .*).

● Close-ended questions needed to be used sparingly or else they make the conversation sound more like a cross-examination. They are useful for keeping wafflers under control, and usually begin with: *would, could, should, do, did, are, has, have.*

● Some useful methods of questioning are:
  - assumptive – '*I imagine your business is . . .*'
  - alternative – '*Do you use one printing company or . . .*'
  - direct – '*How are they handling your requirements . . .*'.

Closing the sale

Always talk confidently about your product and be knowledgeable. Explain what results they'll get, be specific and offer guarantees. If offering a computer repair service, for example, say you return all calls within three hours – guaranteed. *But never promise more than you can deliver.*

Welcome objections as it shows a person is interested, but needs more information.

When customers raise objections it shows they're interested, but need more convincing that your product or service is the one for them. If they say, '*It sounds a lot of money*', break the cost down. If they're considering buying a deluxe motorised bed, for example, which is guaranteed for 30 years, break the cost down to a per night figure. For example: 30p a night, or £2.10 per week, for something that will keep them fitter and healthier and give them a great night's sleep, sounds much more reasonable than something which costs in excess of £3,000. Sandwich it between the benefits by going on to explain how it can actually save them money by reducing the time they have off work with back problems.

The person you are calling is seeking evidence that you can do what they need, so if they say, '*Can you service trucks?*' ask which type of trucks they have and reassure them with your knowledge.

When they choose to do business with you it will be because they believe you do what you do well, so you need to gain their trust.

One of the most common objections is, *'Your price is too high.'* Ask them what they're comparing your prices to and check whether it really is such good value. Perhaps delivery is extra with the model they're comparing it with, or it doesn't come with such a lengthy guarantee. Perhaps the quality of the product is lower or it's only a basic model. The other may not be such a good deal as it sounds. Or perhaps someone really does want your product, but simply can't afford to buy it outright at this time. In this instance you may be able to arrange credit.

When the person doesn't have any more questions, you'll know it's time to close the sale. Lead the person carefully through the ordering process and ask for the order. You can say things such as: *When would you like it delivered?* Or: *All I need now is payment – would you like to pay by cheque, credit card or shall I invoice you?*

If, for whatever reason, the person you called is not buying, respect that. It may be that someone really is offering a better deal than you this time, but there's nothing to stop you contacting your prospect some months down the line with your new and improved product or service.

Heed your customer's requests

A certain way to lose business is to fail to respond to your customer's requests. If they ask you for more information and you fail to send it, they won't bother to ask again. They'll believe that if you can't be relied upon to send information, you can't be relied upon to provide them with the product or service they need.

Existing customers will already have some sort of relationship with you. If you've handled their wants well, most of your contact will be positive. If you phone them, they feel special, they'll know you care about their business and, in the main, welcome your call. If not, respect their wishes and make notes. Perhaps you called at a bad time – make a note of it, or maybe you hadn't done your homework and called them about a totally inappropriate product. But remember, although you try, you can't please everybody.

When making sales calls
Do

- Introduce yourself immediately.
- Project a smiling image.

- Speak distinctly – not too fast.
- Animate your voice.
- Be enthusiastic.
- Keep to the point.
- Be sincere.
- Be a good listener.
- Be interested in what they're saying.
- Sell your ideas.
- Know when to shut up.

Don't

- Waffle on.
- Speak in a monotonous tone.
- Use a special telephone voice.
- Be negative.
- Obstruct your mouth.
- Use jargon.
- Be antagonistic.
- Interrupt.
- Allow yourself to be distracted.
- Sound anxious.
- Knock your competition.

TELEPHONE TIPS

Free calls and Lo-Calls

Many companies now choose to offer a freephone telephone number for taking orders. This does increase response, even on expensive items, where you might consider that the purchaser wouldn't worry about the cost of a phone call. One small printing company mailed all their existing customers A4 laser-printed order forms (with the customer's name and details already overprinted) and put their free order line fax number at the top. The well-thought-out form generated many new sales and was proved to have encouraged their existing customers to continue ordering from them as opposed to going to competitors.

British Telecom (BT) say that more and more people would like to do business by phone. BT now offer Freefone, Lo-Call, Nationalcall and Valuecall numbers and you can contact BT Business Connections on Freefone 0800 800 800 to find out more about the advantages of each. These telephone numbers do significantly increase response, so use them in advertisements, directories, letterheads and business cards. Where applicable, put the number on your product, packaging, company vehicles, invoices and other stationery.

Using an agency

If you don't have the time or simply can't face the idea of ringing people yourself, a telemarketing agency can handle your calls for you. Stormark are one such agency who are happy to deal with small businesses and the self-employed. Whether you have just 10 clients whom you want called on a regular basis, or whether you want to contact 50 people with a view to setting up a meeting, for instance, they can help.

You might consider using such an agency if you're a computer software developer, for example, in the final stages of product development. You're great at what you do, but loathe the idea of getting on the telephone to complete necessary market research. A telemarketing company can ring 50 potential customers and set up face-to-face meetings for you with decision-makers or ask them to complete questionnaires. In the case of the latter you might get as many as 95 per cent of those contacted agreeing to complete the questionnaires.

These are just some of the options open to you. Most agencies give you help with ideas on ways to get your business off the ground and increase your sales.

Keep within the law

The government has finally banned companies from making cold calls (or sending unsolicited faxes) to individuals registered with their two new mandatory opt-out schemes. Now if you breach the regulations by ringing (or faxing) someone who has chosen to opt out of receiving *unsolicited* sales and marketing calls, you could face action by the Data Protection Registrar and fines of up to £5,000 for acting unlawfully.

Call the Telephone and Fax Preference Service on (01932) 414161 for further details and they will send you an information pack.

Useful points to remember

- If you don't answer the phone within 5 rings (8 seconds), 87 per cent of callers will ring your competition.

- If you run the same ad as your competitor, and yours has a freephone number, they'll call you first.

- Handling calls badly can lose you up to 70 per cent of potential business.

- Set up a customer careline – 86 per cent of people think they're useful.

- The listener will retain only about 50 per cent of any telephone conversation, so repetition of key points is necessary.

More useful tips
- Call your own company to see how well they handle your call.

- Ask callers how they heard about you (and record and act upon their responses).

- Re-route calls when lines are busy.

- Start your calls with a verbal handshake – develop rapport.

- Don't keep customers on hold without going back to them frequently – offer to ring them back.

- Transfer the caller to the person who can help *first* time.

- If you ask for information, explain why you need it.

- Make a tape of one of your telephone conversations to highlight areas you can improve.

- Treat every call as different and every caller as unique.

- Acknowledge information you're given and check your understanding.

- Always leave your customer satisfied.

KEY POINTS
- The telephone offers great opportunities for the small business.

- Make telephone contact a priority.

- Follow-up calls increase a mailshot's effectiveness.

- Freephone order lines improve response.

- Develop excellent telephone skills.

8

Powerful Low-Cost, No-Cost Marketing

GETTING YOUR BUSINESS ONLINE

Ultimately, if your company doesn't have a website, you won't have a business.

> Bob Fuller, chief operating officer of Orange

More and more businesses are realising the true potential of having their own website. The UK is now at the forefront of the Internet in Europe. With the Internet offering such enormous potential for any size of business, the importance of being online can't be over-estimated. There are millions of Internet users in the United Kingdom and the number of people going online is rising rapidly. By the year 2005, analysts say that over 25 million people in the UK will be online.

Go online

To go online you need to use an Internet Service Provider (ISP). This used to mean paying a set monthly fee to your chosen provider, but many Internet Service Providers are now offering their services for free, including Tesco and Freeserve. This means you pay only for the lines and the calls (all at local call rates).

Once you're online you'll have your own email account making communication fast and easy. You can send a message to anyone in the world with an email facility for the cost of a local phone call. To retrieve the messages you're sent, you connect to your ISP's server, using your chosen password, at any time of day or night.

Email is a fast way to connect with your customers and suppliers. It allows you to get straight to the point without getting sidetracked and wasting time, but don't let this dominate the way you communicate. A personal phone call or a face-to-face conversation is preferable on many occasions. One of the things which people cite as being stressful in the workplace is receiving masses of email which either isn't necessary or really would have been better said in person.

Don't become one of the growing number of people who are guilty of writing things in an email that they wouldn't say face-to-face.

Your own web pages

The world wide web (www) is a great new marketplace in which you can trade. When you have your own web page, you display your products and services not only to a local, UK or European market, but to a worldwide one. Offer an overview on everything you sell, and even have an online ordering facility. People won't be using the Internet just for purchasing consumer goods – many businesses make lots of money through business-to-business activity, and much more will be made.

The Internet is used by young and old, of every social group, every day. And it appeals to busy, young affluent people who, according to British Telecom, represent the ideal market for telephone sales.

Web page design

Even if you are an experienced computer user, unless you know about Hyper Text Markup Language (HTML) and the different protocols, your website design is best left to someone experienced in these matters. There are many software programs which help you design your own web page, but if you really haven't got the time or the inclination, it's more cost-effective to pay a professional to do it for you. This is usually done for a set fee, plus a monthly servicing fee if you want the information on your site updated as and when necessary. These are all things you need to establish before you start. If you do want someone to update your site, the charges will be in line with the amount of work they need to do every month. If you want to change pictures of products (because the products you're showing have sold, for instance) this will involve either you or the servicer taking new photos and updating text and images on the site.

By putting your website address on adverts, people can browse through what you have to offer at their leisure. They can see more of what you have to offer and, if you've included plenty of information, gain a much better appreciation of how you can benefit them. You can include pictures of you, your products, your staff and testimonials from satisfied customers. Remember to choose your words with care as you would when writing any promotional or advertising material. Have a browse on the Internet, see which sites you find the most user friendly and pick up some tips. That way you'll have a much better idea of what you want when you come to discuss the design of your own site.

Internet shopping

The UK e-commerce market is now worth over a billion pounds, and is predicted to rise to around £18 billion by 2005. The British are already accustomed to buying books, CDs and videos through the Internet, as the success of Internet retailer Amazon.com illustrates. You can log on to their website (*http://www.Amazon.co.uk* or *http://www.Amazon.com*) and search for a book by putting in the *author*, *title* or *subject* or browse by category. If you search in the category *Business and Finance,* for example, the book you are reading now will come up along with other titles. There are also related links – for instance, if you click on the *author's* name, the links will then take you to a list of other books by the same author.

There's no denying that the Internet is an increasingly important part of people's lives and used correctly, is a relatively low-cost way of getting more business. However, never lose sight of what you do with it. Flashy graphics will never replace great customer service and selling the right products and services.

> **How else could you place a virtual full-colour catalogue in front of a worldwide audience for no other cost than your time and a few local telephone calls?**

BECOME NEWSWORTHY

A low-cost way to get publicity is to make yourself newsworthy. Every day, editors and journalists are looking for stories to fill their newspapers, magazines and a wide range of publications. Your local press is a great place to start sending material as their readers are keen to know what others in the locality are up to. So, what makes news?

Taking on new staff
If you've just recruited a new member or members of staff, let the local and trade press know.

You or a member of staff have achieved something
This can be anything from winning a local marathon to giving birth to triplets or receiving an MBE. Don't take for granted what you or your colleagues do.

Outstanding customer service

Hopefully your customer will report this one. If not, you can reveal how you (or one of your staff):

- saved a customer's home from being burgled

- saved their pet dog from drowning

- delivered portable gas fires and camping stoves to customers until long after midnight to ensure they didn't go cold and hungry during a recent powercut.

Anniversaries and milestones

- You trade successfully for 10 years.

- Your business has been in the family for 100 years.

- You serve your 1,000th customer.

- Your 100th client gets the red-carpet treatment.

- You receive your 10th industry award.

- Your partner retires after 25 years.

- You watch your 1,000,000th vase coming off the production line.

Launching a new product or service

- You extend your range to include a new....

- Your service now incorporates....

- You make an invaluable new aid for the disabled.

- You design a gadget which cuts cooking time in half.

- You produce the first ever completely automatic toothpaste dispenser.

Business is booming

- Your sales have quadrupled – good news for local trade, jobs and economy.

- Your sales have reached an all-time high.

- Your product goes worldwide and consumers in the USA, Australia or wherever can't get enough.

- You're so busy, your staff can have as much overtime as they want.

- You're moving to bigger and better premises.

- You've clinched the best ever contract.

Sponsoring
- You sponsor a local amateur dramatic society's production or football team.

- You place and maintain trees in a park or precinct.

- You sponsor a local youth group's evening or outing for the youngsters.

- You sponsor a local boys' band by offering them a place to practise.

Being nice
- You make vases and give some to the local hospital.

- You make chairs and give some to a local hospice.

- You give a selection of books to local schools.

Other ideas
- A celebrity is unveiling your new product or opening your new premises.

- A well-known company has endorsed your innovative business idea.

The ideas are limitless once you get thinking along publicity lines. However, do make sure you send only those stories which you think are truly of interest to the community or trade. A thinly disguised attempt to get free publicity with a weak or thin storyline will be recognised immediately.

Preparing your press release
The format takes many forms, but in general:

- The words *Press Release* need to be printed large and possibly in a colour (red or blue seem to be favourite) at the top of an A4 sheet of paper.

- Underneath to one side you can type the word *Embargo* in your standard letter print size, followed by the date on which (or after which) the news can be released.

- A little further down the page you need to centre your headline (larger print and bolder).

- Type your story in your normal letter size type.

- Use double spacing.

- Write in short paragraphs.

- Use concise language and keep directly to the point.

- Try to keep to under two pages.

- Put the total number of words at the end.

- Put your contact details in full at the end (name and address, telephone and fax numbers and email address).

- Put a footer on each page showing your name and headline.

- Send to a named person.

- Include a photo (see guidelines below).

Photographs
It is preferable to send a photograph provided it is a good one. Most local and regional newspapers print in black and white, so black and white photos are accepted. Try to get prints in an 8″ × 6″ size and write your details on a label and stick on the reverse of the photo in case it detaches itself from your press release. In general, people like pictures of people, so put yourself or your staff in the picture whenever possible, and make sure everyone smiles and looks friendly.

If you haven't any photographs, now could be a good time to consider calling a photographer. Look at examples of their previous work, make sure they know exactly what you want to achieve, and get prices for everything, including developing and reprints.

If this all seems too much for you, take heart. If your story is really newsworthy, the paper will send a photographer to you. You can buy prints from them for other promotions after the story has run.

Writing
You need to hone your writing skills if necessary and submit a neat

accurate typescript. Although a good headline will get the editor or news team interested, they often change it. Write short paragraphs, keeping to the point throughout. Imagine you're the editor – what would your readers want? The biggest mistake is to write hollow material which is obviously no more than a glorified advertisement. No matter how great your story, its publication will depend on what else is in the news at the time. If there's not much going on, you may have a prime spot devoted to you. If there's an all-out strike at the local factory after threats of mass redundancies and a court drama involving a local corrupt official, your chances will be reduced.

Don't be daunted if your first press release doesn't appear. Be patient, keep submitting and follow up with a phone call every so often. If you really can't face the prospect of writing your own press releases, consider hiring a copywriter to prepare them for you. Alternatively call a journalist at the paper – if they think your news is interesting enough they may cover it themselves.

PUBLISHING YOUR OWN NEWSLETTER

Newsletters are a great way of keeping in touch with current customers, past customers, prospects, suppliers – anyone who does business with you. Newsletters are friendly, informative and let people know you haven't forgotten about them. They're great for raising awareness, improving customer relations and getting more business.

Small- and medium-sized businesses, huge corporations, charities, groups, individuals and organisations all produce newsletters and their content and aim vary greatly. Most are produced as a way of maintaining contact within certain groups – friends of a charity, or customers of a particular company, for example. You can use them in all or just some of these ways.

Looks and costs

Your budget will obviously influence many decisions about your newsletter – its size, format, colour, numbers printed, distribution method and more. Sometimes a tighter budget means you waste less money. A newsletter can be anything from an A4 double-sided sheet to a multipage document. Some are produced in black and white and photocopied, others are printed on glossy paper in full colour at great expense. Most small businesses have the facility to run off black and white double-sided copies; if not, a local copy shop can do so at a reasonable cost. Once you see how effective your newsletter is, you may want to invest more, using two colours, for example, and four pages instead of two.

Subscription
Many businesses offer their newsletters on a subscription basis. This not only helps towards the cost of sending and producing, but depending on your subscription price, can soon go into profit. People will be far less inclined to subscribe, however, until they've seen a copy and found it useful and interesting. If you're going to charge, you have to ensure the reader gets their money's worth. Consider offering a free trial period, such as *three months completely free,* and offer money-back guarantees.

Advertising
Your own newsletter is an ideal place for you to promote your products and services. But don't make it too you-oriented or your reader will switch off. There's nothing to stop you accepting advertisements from other companies or individuals who would like to reach your mailing list. Consider people with products and services which complement yours and approach them. This is a good way to get your costs down.

Timing and delivery
How often you send your newsletter is a personal thing. Your budget will determine the answer initially. Many are produced monthly, quarterly or biannually. If your products are seasonal or if you have time-sensitive news, ensure it reaches the reader in plenty of time. The summer is generally a poor time for sending direct mail and newsletters to other businesses. When someone returns from their holiday to find a pile of mail waiting for them, they probably won't have time to read your newsletter, no matter how much they enjoy it. You will need to exercise your judgement on timing.

Your newsletter can be distributed in different ways. You can hand it to people who come into your premises or to people you visit. You can post it either on its own or with your monthly invoices or letters to save postage. You can have it inserted into catalogues or ask other companies if they'll distribute it with their material for a fee. Look at all the options before making a decision.

Keep in touch
A newsletter is a great way of keeping in touch with existing

customers. If you sell vitamins and health products, for example, keep your customers up to date with trends, statistics and information. If they are customers already, they are obviously concerned about their health and actively taking steps to lead a healthy life. Articles in your newsletter will keep them up to date with things which directly interest them. If you mention an article where Vitamin B is recommended, you can refer to the benefits of the Vitamin B tablets you supply.

The *Packaging Digest* is a newsletter produced by a packaging consultancy group which is sent to clients and prospective clients. The newsletter contains important information about packaging legislation and shows how new laws affect the reader. By focusing upon different packaging issues in each edition, such as Returnable Transit Packaging (RTPs), they address readers' concerns.

By keeping people up to date in this way, the Packaging Management Group are providing a valuable service. They demonstrate a real understanding of how the packaging industry works which their readers find reassuring, and, as case histories reveal how they find innovative and cost-effective solutions to a wide variety of clients' packaging problems, the *Packaging Digest* undoubtedly brings in much business.

Points to remember
Your newsletter must be:

- aimed clearly at the reader, and relevant

- easy to read – use lots of pull out quotes, fact boxes and bullet points

- interesting – otherwise it won't get read

- friendly – consider writing a personal note from the editor (you)

- visually interesting – use graphs to highlight trends and comparisons; pictures of people and illustrations or graphics

- uncluttered – don't use lots of different typefaces, or lots of bitty graphics.

If you choose not to produce your own newsletter, consider advertising in someone else's.

EDUCATING YOUR CUSTOMERS

People know they've got to eat, so selling a loaf of bread is easier than selling someone a solution to their lifestyle problems, for instance. The latter may be far more beneficial to them, but the immediate benefits are not quite so clear cut. If you eat bread you satisfy your hunger – it's quick, cheap and easy. The same can't always be said of changing an undesirable lifestyle, although the rewards are potentially far greater.

For this reason it is more difficult to sell some products and services without first giving people information. Advertising the major benefit so it appeals to the reader is a start, but sometimes the product *appears* to be so far removed from the benefit that it lacks credibility.

What people need is not always what they want

You probably know, for example, that relaxation is good for you, but do you understand just how good it is for you? Do you know that in many instances, relaxation can help lower blood pressure and heart rate, alleviate neck, back and headaches, relieve indigestion, and prevent those sickly trembly feelings you might sometimes get? Combatting stress using a variety of techniques, which include relaxation, could prevent major health risks, such as a heart attack or breakdown, or even premature death.

The owner of a small training company, specialising in stress awareness for private and corporate clients, recognises that if she can get clients to practise regular relaxation techniques and make positive life-enhancing changes to their lifestyle, they can live healthier and longer lives. If she advertised the service in this way, however, the claim might be perceived as wild and far-fetched. Besides, if their client is living a high-stress damaging lifestyle, they would also be advised to take many other steps to improve their life expectancy. However, relaxation is a start, a step in the right direction, and will inevitably lead the client to make calmer, better decisions about the way they're living.

Making their need their want

So, although a stressed person doesn't want to buy an aid to relaxation, they do want to live longer, be healthy, feel good about themselves and earn well. Directly and indirectly, relaxation can play a part in all those things. The healthier someone is, the less time they have off work, the more they earn, the better they feel about themselves and so on – a continuing positive cycle. In discovering ways to educate people about what it is you offer, you can turn what they need into what they actually want.

Moving away or towards

People are either motivated towards something or away from it. At some level everyone has *towards* and *away from* motivation – they move towards pleasure and comfort, for instance, and away from pain and discomfort. However, everyone tends to veer more towards one than the other. Imagine a woman who can't bear her job. It's stressful, her immediate superior moans at her continually, and the hours are unsociable. A *moving away* type of person won't do anything about it until they really can't stand it any more. The moving *towards* type of person is motivated to actively seek another job, and quickly, because she wants to do something more fulfilling and rewarding.

The stress trainer mentioned above must consider this when she's preparing her promotional material, as *moving towards* type people will actively seek ways to improve their health and lifestyle. *Moving away* type people, however, will only do so if the threat of something more awful is put before them – pain or premature death, for example.

Getting into print

There are many ways you can do this, and some have already been featured. Advertisements, direct mail and newsletters are good examples. In a newsletter, for example, you can give more background to your products and services. Not only is this good for your business, it makes your readers feel more knowledgeable and, human nature being what it is, they'll pass it on to others, to show how much they know. If you don't produce your own newsletter, see if you can get a regular column in someone else's. They might be only too pleased to offer their readers your expert view.

Tune in to radio

If you're a specialist in a particular field, why not consider having a weekly, monthly or one-off spot on a radio station? Local radio stations would be a good place to contact first. Make your proposal interesting, and come up with aspects which really will interest their listeners. Don't approach them with the intention of directly promoting yourself and your business.

If you are an antique dealer, for instance, your local radio station may think it's a great idea to give you a spot on their afternoon show. They might give you four spots which you could schedule as follows:

Week 1 How To Care For Your Antiques
Week 2 How To Recognise A Fake
Week 3 How To Spot Hidden Treasures
Week 4 Answer Listeners' Questions

By letting people know how they can increase the value of their antiques, how to care for grandfather's clock, and the importance of choosing a respected restorer to undertake work, listeners would learn a great deal. The dealer would be introduced by name: Rosemary Reynolds, proprietor of Maxfield House, for example.

Educating your prospects in this way has many advantages:

- it builds your profile
- it raises public awareness of your specialist area
- it raises your credibility
- and you are perceived as an expert in your field.

One Berkshire-based business consultant secured himself a regular series of slots on an early morning drive-time show when many business people were on their way to work. He was 'interviewed' by the programme host about a series of money matters and his name and consultancy were given a mention too. Although the interview appeared spontaneous, it was actually scripted to ensure there were no embarrassing hitches.

Tapes and videos

Consider, too, making an audio tape or video that gives more detailed background information about you, your products and services. The cheaper method is to produce an audio tape which you can either script yourself or get a copywriter to do for you:

- Seven ways to resolve your decorating problems.
- Ten ways to prevent burnout.
- How to hire an accountant who saves you time **and** money.
- Before choosing a new caravan, listen to this....

You could make a small charge for these tapes to cover production costs, or give them to selected prospects. Educate prospective clients and customers, so that they can see:

1. the benefits of using products and services such as yours, *and*

2. why they should choose *your* product or service as opposed to your competitors.

KEY POINTS

- Make worldwide communication fast and easy – go online.
- Trade 24 hours a day, every day of the year with your own website.
- Use newsletters to keep in touch with suppliers and customers.
- Build contacts with your local press.
- Be recognised as an expert in your field.

9

More Ways To Grow Your Business

SEIZE THE OPPORTUNITIES IN TRENDS

Genetically modified (GM) food is a prime example of an area where businesses saw and seized the opportunity presented by trends. Iceland was the first of the big UK supermarkets to declare itself non-GM in 1998, and none of its own-brand products contain either GM ingredients or derivatives. Iceland intends to remove all artificial additives and colourings from its own label ranges, if they haven't already. Where it's safe to do so, they will remove preservatives too. This is a good example of a company recognising a trend towards healthy eating and responding to it.

Follow the crowd

The media often set and reflect trends. Consider the range of magazines and television and radio programmes devoted to gardening. In 1960s Britain, gardeners typically grew their own vegetables, had a straight concrete path up the middle of the garden, possibly alongside a long washing line, a strip of lawn either side and a few flowers. Today, there are a multitude of new and different products for the garden and gardener – everything from wheely bin covers, solar pond pumps and outdoor lamps, to self-watering planters, kneeling pads, electronic animal scarers, heat-sensitive security lights, and a staggering choice of garden furniture.

One small company, which have made fencing since the early 1970s, now also make bespoke wooden gazebos, pergolas, decking and ornate trellis. They also source and sell related products, including garden statuary and planters. They have more staff, more business and profits have never been better.

Help lead the way

What other trends are emerging? Think how you can grow your business by responding to current trends. When you do identify a growing trend, don't just dismiss it if it doesn't fit in with your current business or thinking, or if it appears totally unrelated. Be

imaginative and think laterally.
Consider the following:

- households where both partners and/or parents work
- what people spend on pets
- people who work from home
- people who travel abroad.

The above rising trends have resulted in a growing number of products and services, including:

- domestic cleaning and maintenance services
- house-sitting services
- pet care products, sitting and walking services
- security products and services.

Security is always at the forefront of people's minds. People want their homes, their loved ones, their cars and their businesses safe. They want personal and financial security too, and time and money-saving products and services are always welcome.

There are 23 million households in the UK alone – an enormous market if you look for trends and respond to them.

Leisure

Much free time is spent on leisure pursuits, gardening and DIY. Again the number of television programmes on home style and decorating reflect a growing trend. People are now far more likely to experiment with decorative paint effects in their home, either as a DIY project or having a professional do it for them. Feng Shui is playing a bigger part in how people design, layout, decorate and furnish their homes. If you manufacture furniture or fittings, perhaps you could design pieces with good Feng Shui in mind.

Health and beauty

More people are taking responsibility for their own well-being and general health. The number of complementary therapists has risen greatly, and people who admit that ten years ago they didn't know what aromatherapy was, now use it regularly. There has been an increase in the number of fitness centres and health clubs, and all the products and services related to them.

> **The aim is to look at growth trends and exploit the opportunities they afford you.**

FINDING OTHER THINGS TO SELL

There are often opportunities to sell other products or services in addition to those you currently offer. Usually, these would be complementary products, depending on your business. Customers are far more likely to buy something extra at the point of purchase than at a later time, so it makes sense to offer your additional items then. This is why electrical goods retailers, for example, try to sell you extended insurance when you buy a new fridge-freezer or television. They know you're far less likely to buy it later.

Extra products and services

If you run a vehicle repair shop, for example, why not offer your customers a same-day valeting service? This way when they pick up their car not only will it run perfectly, it will look great, and it's extra turnover and profit for you.

Do you sell computers? Consider selling computer desks, chairs and associated accessories. If you sell sofas or carpets, ask the customer if they want them treated with stain protectors before delivery. If you make loose covers and curtains, offer cushions for sofas, and duvets and valances to complement bedroom curtains.

One pet-grooming service decided to sell pet products and accessories too. They gave all their customers a brochure showing their new products, together with an order form which they collect from the customer when they pick up their pet. Now when the pets are delivered home after grooming, they arrive with food, supplements, any accessories their owners have ordered *and* a fresh order form. Clients are delighted and appreciate:

- no more lugging heavy sacks of pet food home
- getting all their pet needs from one place at one time
- saving time and effort.

The pet groomers say the pet product side of their business has become more profitable than grooming, and they're considering expanding into pet-sitting and walking services. They have built up an enviable reputation with their customers, who regularly recommend others.

One of the things their customers also enjoy is free advice about common pet problems. This is because the owners have made it their business to learn as much as possible about the animals they care for, which they say allows them to offer a rounded, satisfying service to all their customers.

> **Remember the key is to offer the additional or upgraded service at the time of ordering or purchase as this is when the customer is most likely to buy.**

JOINING FORCES

The joy of joining forces with another business, whatever its size, is that everyone benefits – you, the other business and your customers.

For example, a sports shop owner contacts a local holiday park, which has its own heated indoor swimming pool and health club, and asks if it has any quiet periods. The holiday park proprietor explains that from October to April the pool is hardly used. The sports shop owner strikes a deal with the park owner whereby he can buy six-month memberships for that period at a token fee. The sports shop then advertises *'Six Months Free Health Club Membership Worth £150, With Every £150 Spent!'* and sales soar. The holiday park enjoys more members than ever during what is a usually quiet period and are thrilled when over 50 per cent of them pay the full fee to join the club for another year.

Recommendation

Another great way to get extra business is to recommend associated professions or suppliers. Graphic designers use printing services, and printers have clients who need help with design. It makes sense to formalise an arrangement where each of them recommend the other's services and in return receive a percentage of the customer's total spend. The designer could advertise printing as a part of his services, and the printers can offer design services as part of theirs.

> **Whenever you recommend another business, you must be confident that they will provide an outstanding service or product in the same way that you do. If not, it will reflect on you, and you could lose a valuable customer.**

SELLING YOUR OWN ADVERTISING SPACE

There are many ways in which you can advertise the services and products of other businesses. You could advertise a business which supplies you, or offers complementary products or associated services. You could even advertise unrelated products and services, provided they don't appear at complete odds with your own ethos and business.

You could:

- include their leaflet or brochure in with your monthly invoices, mailshot or catalogue
- print their advert on the back of your invoices
- place their advert in your company newsletter
- print an advert for them in your catalogue.

You need to establish how many people would see or read the advertisement. If you're sending out a mailshot to 10,000 horse owners, for example, and you know of an insurance company which has special deals on horse, rider and buildings insurance, ask them if they want to include a brochure or leaflet. In addition to the charge you make for doing this, you could agree to take a percentage of the business they get as a result.

In the picture

When you take photographs of your products for adverts, brochures or catalogues, consider involving another company's products. If you produce ceramics, for example, approach a furniture manufacturer. They might be keen to have your ceramics displayed on their furniture. A picture showing your vases on their side tables, together with their contact details somewhere in the brochure, would be a good advertisement for them if going to enough of the right people.

Formalise the arrangement, ensure the service and products of those businesses you advertise are outstanding, and deal only with people you trust.

DISCOVER HIDDEN ASSETS

In the day-to-day running of your business you probably take for granted many of the assets you have. At times these assets may be in full use, and at other times under-used. This can vary from season to season, order to order, and depend on a wide range of factors. Unless every aspect of your business is running to full capacity, you could be wasting money. That's why it pays to look at ways of fully utilising all your assets and resources.

- **Excess space**. Do you have space which is not being used? Could you offer it to other companies who want short- or longer-term storage space? Or how about one of the growing numbers of home workers who need extra storage space? One small business had a basic agricultural-style building standing empty in their yard. Now they let it to a plumbing partnership who use it to store equipment and reclaimed sinks and baths.

- **Vehicles**. How often does your van travel empty? How many times does your truck make an outbound or return journey without a load? Maybe you make a certain trip regularly to another part of the country or you're planning a one-off trip somewhere. A telecommunications consultant used to drive from Plymouth to London several times a week in his empty estate car. Now, at least once a week, he delivers hand-decorated glass to a specialist gift shop near his destination in the capital.

- **Equipment capacity**. Does your factory or office machinery work to its full capacity? Do you have quiet periods between contracts? Who else would benefit from using your equipment? A state-of-the-art laser printer and binding machine was a worthwhile investment for one surveying team. They produced their own brochures, printed their own mailshots and bound reports complete with covers. When they heard that a neighbouring environmental consultant took his reports across town to be printed and bound at a copy shop, they offered their facilities, which were more convenient and cheaper.

- **Staff**. Do you have quiet periods? Do you or your staff have lulls at certain times of the year? Or perhaps you're in a business where it's all go one minute, and quiet the next. A tool manufacturer's graphic designer was employed full time, but invariably had quiet periods, usually after hectic deadlines were met. The company owner discovered that one of his customers wished to redesign her product's packaging. Now he sells her the services of his own graphic designer (at quiet times) at a special rate.

Whatever equipment, machinery or resources you have, ask yourself if you're utilising them to their full capacity. Check with insurance and other interested parties to ensure you're meeting your legal obligations. If additional costs are involved, pass these on to the person you're sharing your resources with, as it will still be more cost-effective for them than setting up their own infrastructure or equipment.

Other advantages

In most instances there are added advantages to maximising your assets in this way. Imagine you own the tool company in the above graphic design example. The added benefit to you is that in getting your customers' packaging designed well, their sales will increase, which means they'll need to buy more (and more often) from you.

The networking aspects of this cannot be ignored either. Your willingness to consider the problems your customers, suppliers and other businesses face, and to come forward with solutions, will undoubtedly be greatly appreciated. Where your own customers are involved it shows great customer service.

So, if this is an area which you haven't considered before, don't make false assumptions or put unnecessary obstacles in the way – find out first. Be a possibility thinker!

KEY POINTS

- Recognise and respond to trends.
- Be imaginative and think laterally.
- Sell associated products and services.
- Offer more when people order or purchase.
- Advertise other businesses – profitably.
- Fully utilise *all* your assets and resources.

Glossary

Advertorial. Advertisement laid out to resemble editorial.

AIDCA. Attention, Interest, Desire, Conviction, Action.

Body copy. The main area of copy in an advertisement, letter and other written material.

Business mailing. Sending mailings to people at their business addresses.

Cold calling. Contacting people who are not known to have bought from the advertiser.

Consumer mailing. Sending mailings to consumers at home addresses.

Copy. Words used to promote people, products and services.

Copywriter. Person who writes copy for advertisements, mailings and promotions.

Customer profile. Collection of facts about a customer.

Database. Records of customers, prospects, products, any information held in a retrieval system – usually on computer.

Demographics. Socio-economic facts about customers.

Direct mail. Advertising sent through post (usually to a named individual).

E-commerce. Trade done on the Internet.

Email. Electronic mail.

Flyer. A single unfolded sheet of promotional material.

Follow-up. A letter or phone call following previous contact.

Freepost. Service offered by the Royal Mail whereby people can respond to your advertisements without paying postage.

Fulfilment house. A company which handles fulfilment of your orders, from handling response to sending products and collecting payment.

Graphic designer. A professional artist who designs promotional material.

gsm. Grams per square metre (a way of measuring paper weight).

Headline. Opening of advertisement or mailshot which is larger and bolder than body copy.

HTML. Hyper Text Markup Language.

Inserts. Advertisement leaflets (or similar) either inserted loosely or stitched into a magazine.

ISP. Internet Service Provider.

List broker. Specialist who rents and sells lists of names and addresses of individuals or companies (subdivided into numerous categories).

List building. Gathering names and addresses for marketing purposes.

List cleaning. Correcting incorrect details.

Mail order. Ordering (and paying) for products through the post.

Mailing list. Names and addresses of people you send mailshots to.

Mailshot. Advertising sent through the post, usually to a named individual.

Media. Carriers of advertising, including radio, television and newspapers.

MOPS. Mail Order Protection Scheme.

Proof. Draft of printed material for checking.

Prospects. People who are not yet customers.

Response. Replies to your advertising.

Source code. Code put on advertisements and in return addresses which allows advertiser to check which promotional activity generated the response.

Target audience. Defined group of prospects.

Telemarketing. Using the telephone to market, using incoming and outgoing calls.

USP. Unique Selling Proposition.

www. World wide web.

Useful Addresses

Advertising Standards Authority
2 Torrington Place
London WC1E 7HW
Tel: (020) 7580 5555

The Direct Marketing Association
Haymarket House
1 Oxendon Street
London SW1Y 4EE
Tel: (020) 7321 2525
Fax: (020) 7321 0191

Fax Preference Service (FPS)
(Address as Telephone Preference Service below)
Tel: (020) 7766 4422
Fax: (020) 7976 1886
Website: *www.dma.org.uk*

Institute of Direct Marketing
1 Park Rd
Teddington
Middlesex TW11 0AR
Tel: (020) 8977 5705

Mailing Preference Service (MPS)
5 Reef House
Plantation Wharf
London SW13 3UF
Tel: (020) 7738 1625

Mail Order Protection Scheme (MOPS)
16 Took's Court
London EC4A 1LB

Tel: (020) 7405 6806
Fax: (020) 7404 0106

The Market Research Society (MRS)
15 Northburgh Street
London EC1V 0AH
Tel: (020) 7490 49111

Royal Mail Products and Services
Your local sales centre: 0345 950 950

Sallyann Sheridan
Marketing Copywriter
All About You
PO Box 3767
Bridport
DT6 6RX
Email: sallyann@allabout-you.com
Tel: (01404) 43300

Stormark Telemarketing
Stormark House
30a Horsefair
Banbury
Oxon OX16 0AE
Tel: (01295) 268143
Fax: (01295) 268149
Website: *www.stormark.ltd.uk/telemarketing*

Telephone Preference Service (TPS)
Haymarket House
1 Oxendon Street
London SW1Y 4EE
Tel: (020) 7766 4420
Fax: (020) 7976 1886
Website: *www.dma.org.uk*

Information about Data Protection Act 1998 is available from:

The Stationery Office
Tel: 0870 600 5522
or via the Internet at:

Data Protection Act 1998 – *www.parliament.uk*

Data Protection: The Government's Proposals – *www.homeoffice. gov.uk/datap1.htm*

EU Data Protection Directive (95/46/EC) – *www2.echo.lu/legal/en/ dataprot/dataprot.html*

Data Protection Act 1984 – *www.open.gov.uk/dpr/dprhome.htm*

Further Reading

Cash Flows and Budgeting Made Easy, third edition, Peter Taylor (How To Books, 2000).
Ogilvy on Advertising, David Ogilvy (Guild Publishing).
Profit Through The Post, Alison Cork (Piatkus).
Think And Grow Rich, Napoleon Hill.
Writing Great Copy, Sallyann Sheridan (How To Books, 1999).

Index

STARTING A BUSINESS FROM HOME
All the ideas and advice you need to run a profitable venture

Graham Jones

The fourth edition of this popular book contains a wealth of ideas, projects, tips, facts, checklists and quick-reference information. With advice on everything from choosing a good business idea and starting to advertise, to book-keeping and dealing with professionals, this book is basic reading for every budding entrepreneur. 'This book is essential – full of practical advice.' *Home Run.*

176pp. illus. 1 85703 492 9. 4th edition.

BECOMING A CONSULTANT
How to start and run a profitable consulting business

Susan Nash

Consulting has become a lucrative and growing working option. This book will provide you with the methodology to set up and run your own consulting business and an understanding of the steps you need to take to make it successful. It will enable you to define your business's strategic direction and give you the practical skills to make your business a reality. You will learn how to raise finances, maintain financial control, implement a marketing strategy and deliver on-going business. Susan Nash is the British President of EM-Power, a US based consulting firm which has worked with over 50 companies in both the UK and USA. She has presented the workshop 'Consulting and Making Money At It', for the past seven years.

144pp. illus. 1 85703 392 2.

MAKING DIRECT MAIL WORK
How to boost your profits with effective direct mail promotion

Peter Arnold

Direct mail is a proven and effective method of promotion for almost every type of organisation, large or small. Love it or hate it, direct mail works. Any small company, or even self-employed people, can take advantage of this most flexible and controllable of all promotional media. This book sets out, in a simple and graphic way, exactly how to initiate and run your own direct mail system. It also shows you how to avoid the pitfalls and maximise effectiveness and efficiency. Peter Arnold has been creating and writing direct mail campaigns for over 35 years, and is one of the most experienced professionals in Britain. He has worked for every sort of organisation from the large multinational to the one and two-man operation.

120pp. illus. 1 85703 297 7.

WRITING A PRESS RELEASE
How to get the right kind of publicity and news coverage

Peter Bartram

Which stories make an editor sit up and take notice? Why do some press releases never get used? This book explains all. 'Takes you step-by-step through the process.' *Home Run Magazine.* 'Shows how to style and build a news story that carries value for readers...I recommend this book.' *Writers Forum.* 'Yes! Here at last is a book that tells it like it is.' Phoenix, Association of Graduate Careers Advisory Services.

144pp. illus. 1 85703 485 6. 3rd edition.

TAKING UP A FRANCHISE
How to buy and run a successful franchised business

Matthew Record

The success rate for a franchised business currently stands at an impressive eight out of ten. However before you consider buying a franchise you should know all that is involved: the financial commitment, the franchisor/franchisee obligations, the potential pitfalls, the chances of success. This book seeks to equip you with everything you need to know in order to select, buy and run a successful franchised business. Matthew Record is a business consultant, specialising in the preparation of business plans for a variety of commercial clients. He is author of *Preparing a Winning Business Plan*, also in this series.

128pp. illus. 1 85703 484 8.

SETTING UP A LIMITED COMPANY
How to form and operate a company as a director and shareholder

Robert Browning

Limited liability represents a responsibility to the general public and gives business dealings a public face. Directors, too, have onerous responsibilities. This book has been written by Robert Browning, a chartered accountant formerly in public practice with many years' experience of small businesses. It sets out simply how to decide whether a company is right for you and, if so, how to go about it. Apart from a detailed explanation of how to form a company, it covers the filing of statutory information, the opening of bank accounts, taxation, wages and salaries, marketing, auditing and accountancy, and the use of computers.

136pp. illus. 1 85703 452 X. 2nd edition.